Noonan

Career

D0856709

ment

Project

Academia in Transition

Academia in Transition: Mid-Career Change or Early Retirement

Carl V. Patton

University of Illinois at Urbana-Champaign

Abt Books
Cambridge, Massachusetts

Part of this book is based upon material prepared with support of National Science Foundation Contract No. PRM-7624576. The findings expressed here are those of the author and do not necessarily reflect the views of the National Science Foundation.

Library of Congress Catalog Card Number 78-66694

Printed in the United States of America.

ISBN: 0-89011-514-1

To my best friend

Contents

Figures and Tables

LIST OF FIGURES

xiii

LIST OF TABLES

Acknowledgments

I am deeply grateful to the early retirement and mid-career change program administrators and participants who granted us personal interviews. I would also like to acknowledge the contributions of Dr. Joseph Zelan and Diane Kell. Dr. Zelan conducted the research on mid-career change programs and drafted the discussion of the topic in chapter 2. Ms. Kell interviewed the early retirees and drafted the analysis of their responses.

Gretchen West Patton conducted the research on early retirement and mid-career change in the military and civil service. Mr. Robert Lake drafted chapter 6 on the legal implications of early retirement programs, and Mr. Robert Foertsch developed the faculty flow model.

Dr. Carlos Kruytbosch and other representatives of the National Science Foundation gave us support, advice, and assistance throughout the study. Ms. Lenore Bixby, Dr. James D. Bruce, Mr. Mitchell Meyer, Mr. Donald E. Sullivan, and Dr. Dorothy S. Zinberg were members of the project advisory committee.

Other people to whom I am grateful include Dr. Martin A. Trow who provided advice during the formative phase of this research, Dr. Clark Kerr and Dr. Margaret Gordon of the Carnegie Council on Policy Studies in Higher Education and University of California past president Charles J. Hitch, who provided financial support for my early work on retirement, and Ms. Nancy C. Miner who handled the many details in the production of this book.

Academia in Transition

Introduction

PROFESSOR GREEN

For almost thirty years Professor Green was an active, productive member of his department. Early in his career he regularly taught large introductory courses and smaller advanced seminars, and he supervised a number of doctoral candidates. His research was respected; he published regularly; and he held his share of committee assignments, including a stint as chairman of his department.

But things changed in recent years, and Professor Green did not keep pace. New researchers in his field and in his department (some had even been his students) were carrying on experiments that Professor Green had difficulty understanding. The mathematical models were beyond his grasp. As Professor Green admitted, "I was no longer on the forefront of my field; I really hadn't been for quite a while. It was difficult pretending I was."

"My course wasn't popular anymore," he continued. "One quarter no one signed up for it; another time only a handful of students. . . . Mostly I was doing research, but then my grant ran out, and I couldn't find anyone who was interested in funding my work. . . . I felt that I might as well retire; there wasn't much use in going on. There really wasn't much for me to do."

But Professor Green realized he could not retire. Although he had been with the university for many years, he was still three years away from mandatory retirement. If he retired now, his pension would be smaller than the one he would receive if he waited until mandatory retirement. Retiring early would also mean that he would have to live on that reduced pension income for an extra three years. It was out of the question. "I really hadn't thought about retiring before [the mandatory retirement age]. I didn't do anything to plan for it because I hadn't seriously considered retirement until my grants ran out and students were no longer interested in my courses."

About this time, however, Professor Green's university was instituting a special early-retirement arrangement. It had recognized the problems faced by persons like him, and it was also interested in finding ways to open the faculty ranks to younger academics, women, and minorities. So one spring afternoon Professor Green's department chairman spoke to him about an arrangement which would allow him to retire early, with the university making up the shortfall in his pension. "The department chairman brought it up," reported Professor Green. "He suggested that I could fit into the early retirement program. . . . It really wasn't an option." Thus, Professor Green retired several years before he had planned. His early retirement freed him from an unhappy situation while opening the university's ranks to new employees with skills more in demand.

While some universities and colleges have started to experiment with incentive early-retirement options, other universities have begun to explore the feasibility of mid-career change programs. Rather than encouraging academics to retire early, these mid-career change programs attempt to help professors prepare for a career in another field or profession.

Concerned about academia's diminishing ability to hire young scientists, the National Science Foundation sponsored research on alternative incentive early-retirement and mid-career change programs.[1] The investigation had two purposes. The first was to collect information useful to colleges and universities seeking short-run solutions to the staffing problems caused by their slowing growth rate. The second purpose was to assemble information useful to individual academics contemplating early retirement or career change.

What early-retirement and mid-career change options are possible? How effective are they? What are their costs? What does early retirement mean to an academic? These are the basic questions addressed in this book. By examining recently adopted incentive early-retirement and mid-career change programs, we illustrate the many facets of the issue: the dollar costs, the human elements, the legal and administrative aspects, and the potential impact upon the age structure of university faculties.

Interviewed for this study were the administrators of increased benefits early-retirement schemes at the University of California, Colgate University, Indiana University, the Massachusetts Institute of Technology, the University of Pittsburgh, and Stanford University. We also interviewed program administrators from A. E. Staley Manufacturing; American Cyanamid; Bank of America; Campbell Soup; Caterpillar Tractor; Celanese Corporation; Consolidated Edison; Crocker National Bank; Du Pont; Eastman Kodak; Exxon; General Foods; Honeywell; International Business Machines; IU International; International Nickel; J. C. Penney; Metropolitan Life; Monsanto; PPG Industries; Quaker Oats; Security Pacific National Bank; Standard Oil, Indiana; and Westinghouse. Information about the increased benefits early-retirement options of fourteen other firms was obtained from data collected by other researchers.

For information on mid-career change programs, we contacted representatives of all the firms listed above, plus United Airlines, American Airlines, RCA, Lloyds Bank of Los Angeles, and Boeing Aircraft. In addition, a representative of the American Society for Training and Development gave us an overview of training efforts in business and industry. Information was also supplied by the administrators of two fellowship programs: the Economic Policy Fellowships of the Brookings Institution and the Congressional Science and Engineering Fellowships of the American Association for the Advancement of Science. Interviews were conducted with representatives of the State University System of Florida and the Pennsylvania State Colleges system, which are engaged in programs to retrain faculty members for work in new academic fields.

Our information on mid-career change and early retirement in the military and civil service comes from a search of the literature as well as from interviews with representatives of the Department of Defense, the Retired Officers Association, and the House and Senate Armed Services Committees.

THE PLAN OF THE BOOK

Chapter 1 explains why colleges and universities are interested in mid-career change and early-retirement programs, and it outlines the various options now available.

Career options in industry, government, and academia are analyzed in chapter 2. Unfortunately, little is being done in the area of mid-career change programs, although several models exist as possible alternatives. In contrast to this limited experience are industry's long involvement and academia's more recent experience with early retirement schemes. After reviewing this experience, we discuss the military and civil service pension system provisions, believed by some to be useful models for academia.

Since the decision to retire early is such an important personal consideration, chapter 3 is devoted to an analysis of the experiences of seventy of the first hundred or so persons who were induced to retire early. Why did they agree to retire early? Are they satisfied with their decisions? How has early retirement affected their general well-being and professional activity? Looking back, how do these persons evaluate the programs under which they terminated?

Universities and colleges have shown interest in early retirement because they hope, despite severe financial constraints, to find a way to hire new employees with needed skills. One source of expected revenue is the salary line released by the early retiree. Do early-retirement schemes free funds with which to hire new employees? Which are the most cost-effective alternatives? These questions are discussed in chapter 4.

Chapter 5 examines the manpower question. How will incentive early-retirement affect the age distribution of university and college faculties? Can early-retirement and mid-career change programs substantially modify age and talent distributions? Which variables promise the greatest effect? The results of changes in tenure rates, death and retirement rates, outmigration rates, and mid-career change rates are illustrated.

Care must be taken in the design and administration of these programs, especially of incentive early-retirement schemes. Chapter 6 contains a discussion of the funding requirements and tax implications of increased-benefit retirement programs and an analysis of the legal aspects of age discrimination.

In the concluding chapter, we sketch the policy implications of mid-career change and early retirement, present a summary evaluation of the early-retirement schemes, and outline a number of considerations for colleges, universities, and faculty members contemplating these options.

NOTE

1. Carl Vernon Patton, Diane Kell, and Joseph Zelan, "A Survey of Institutional Practices and an Assessment of Possible Options Relating to Voluntary Mid- and Late-Career Changes and Early Retirement for University and College Faculty," mimeographed (Cambridge, MA: Abt Associates, 1977).

1

The Rationale
for Career Options

THE STEADY-STATE

Academia's interest in early retirement and mid-career change programs derives to a large extent from the budgetary and manpower problems now faced by many colleges and universities. During the so-called "steady-state,"[1] some colleges and universities will find that they are able to hire few young professors—the very people upon whom they depend substantially for new ideas and rejuvenation. The problem will be particularly acute for institutions with large percentages of tenured faculty members, schools experiencing slow or no growth, and those having few retirements. These institutions may find that they are unable to respond to enrollment shifts and other changing demands. Furthermore, the steady-state and low turnover may make it difficult for a university to increase the number of women and minority faculty members at a rate it considers desirable.[2]

We will not reanalyze the implications of the steady-state here.[3] Suffice it to say that American higher education is now faced with a decline in college enrollments and other problems that suggest that it will need fewer new faculty members during the next decade at least.[4] Although new students might be recruited, an increase in the demand for new college professors is not expected.[5] Certain institutions are even now having a difficult time supplying their current faculties with students.[6] Some of the less prestigious campuses of the large universities and some of the less selective small colleges may be especially hard-pressed to attract students during the next decade.[7]

University and college administrators have shown the greatest interest in early-retirement and mid-career change options, but these programs may be attractive to faculty members as well. Our research suggests that, over the years, some faculty members (perhaps a small percentage) may become less productive and less interested in teaching, that some may want to undertake different activities before they retire, and that for a variety of reasons some professors desire to change careers or retire earlier than originally planned.

The manpower problem is compounded at many institutions by the relative youth of the professorial force, recruited *en masse* during the education boom of the 1950s and 1960s. Many young professors, hired in their late twenties and early thirties, are at least a decade or two away from retirement. Nonetheless, they may be in fields that are no longer in demand. The work histories of some of the current faculty members exacerbate the problem. Although most faculty members were hired for a variety of purposes—teaching, research, advising students, administration—some of them performed no more than one of these tasks until recent retrenchments required them to shoulder other responsibilities. A few of these persons are unequipped to perform their new duties. For example, because institutions have sought to attract students from groups never before represented on their campuses, some faculty members have been requested to teach nontraditional students in off-campus programs at "inconvenient" times. These new tasks have not been seen as desirable by all who have been asked to do them.[8]

Still another small group of potential candidates for early retirement or career change includes persons who have run out of functions to perform. Although they may have been able to teach, research, administer, advise students, and serve on committees early in their careers, they may now be unable to handle any of these roles. Because the steady-state has affected administrative positions too, these persons cannot be "kicked upstairs." Early retirement or mid-career change might be good for them.

Many problems might be addressed by early-retirement and mid-career change programs. Such arrangements might be used to respond to declining enrollments, changes in knowledge, numerical redundancy (too many faculty members performing the same task), budgetary shortages, the demand for faculty positions for women and minorities, and the need for faculty rejuvenation. Colleges and universities have addressed these problems in other ways, too. Off-campus instruction, evening programs, and the recruitment of new student groups have been undertaken in part to deal with declining enrollments and tight budgets. Issuing one-year renegotiable appointments, employing part-time and visiting faculty members, and leaving faculty vacancies unfilled have also been used to respond to budgetary problems. In order to employ women and minorities, hiring practices have been modified, but this policy can be successful only if faculty positions are available. Sabbaticals are often intended to provide opportunities for faculty rejuvenation. Some faculty members had their teaching and research loads reduced, and their administrative tasks increased, in order to permit persons with more recent academic training to teach and research.

Although these actions respond to somewhat different problems (budgetary decreases and the need for different faculty skills), they are all intended to deal with short-run manpower needs. This is precisely why some persons consider early retirement a desirable academic policy: one action responds to two needs. They see early retirement as a way to reduce costs (or reduce manpower levels) and as a way to open up the faculty ranks to persons with needed academic qualifications and demographic characteristics.

Some persons argue that if tenure were abolished, it would not be necessary to increase the levels of early retirement and mid-career change. Removing tenure, they claim, would permit institutions to remove unproductive faculty members and respond to changing demand. Others argue that making tenure more difficult to obtain would increase turnover and, by reducing the number of persons with permanent claims to positions, would give institutions greater flexibility in responding to changing demands. Although both of these arguments should be, and are being, investigated further, changes in tenure rules would have an effect only in the long run since there would likely be an actual or implied grandfather clause to protect current tenured employees.[9] In fact, these changes would hardly open faculty ranks to new employees.[10] Their main short-run effect would be to increase the competition among junior faculty members for the few entry slots available. Although the long-run effect of eliminating tenure might be desirable, administrators who want to open more faculty slots quickly must look for a different policy.[11]

Most universities have early-retirement provisions as part of their regular retirement plans. Persons who have reached a certain age, and who have contributed to the retirement system for a minimum number of years, may begin to draw an annuity, but less than they would draw if they retired at the mandatory age. For a variety of reasons (basically financial), few persons retire more than a couple of years early under this option. Thus, institutions have considered increased-benefit or incentive early-retirement schemes. Under these arrangements, persons who elect to retire early are provided increased annuities that are, in some cases, as large as those due them at the mandatory retirement age. This financial incentive is intended to encourage more persons to retire early and release their faculty positions sooner than expected.

THE ABOLITION OF MANDATORY RETIREMENT

University and college interest in early retirement has been heightened by recent congressional action which raised the mandatory retirement age. On April 6, 1978, the Age Discrimination in Employment Act of 1967 was amended to extend the mandatory retirement age from 65 to 70 in private industry and nonfederal public employment and to remove it completely for federal employees.[12] The amendment, which received overwhelming support in both the House and Senate, did raise concern among university and corporate officials. These persons feared that the higher mandatory retirement age would reduce their ability to hire new employees. A controversial Senate amendment would have exempted tenured university professors from the higher mandatory retirement age. That is, tenured professors, and tenured professors only, would still have been required to retire at age 65. Administrators and nontenured faculty members, however, could have kept their jobs until age 70. The American Association of University Professors challenged this provision, arguing that it excluded professors with tenure from protection under the Age Discrimination in Employment Act.[13]

Supporters of the exemption argued that eliminating mandatory retirement would make it difficult to weed out the "deadwood" and open the employment ranks to younger persons, women, and minorities. Executives of several major corporations argued that a mandatory retirement age was necessary because it protected workers against unequal treatment by preventing individual retirement decisions based on merit. Administrators also tended to favor mandatory retirement because the fixed age made it easier to plan for pension costs.

The compromise agreed upon by the conference committee defers boosting the mandatory retirement age to 70 for professors until 1982. The purpose of the postponement was to give colleges and universities time to adjust their hiring and tenure policies. In the long run, the mandatory retirement of professors at any age will probably be outlawed. Several congressmen are determined to eliminate mandatory retirement, most notably Claude Pepper of Florida and Jacob Javits of New York. Furthermore, several states, following the lead of California, are moving to prohibit mandatory retirement by state government and private business.

What effect the abolition of mandatory retirement might have is unclear, but the major fear of many university and college administrators is that it would reduce turnover rates and impair their ability to hire young scholars. There are still other reasons for keeping mandatory retirement. It causes persons to plan for the day when they will be unable to work, be it due to poor health, family responsibilities, or dissatisfaction with their job. When a person is young, the idea of not working may be repugnant, and there may be little incentive to save for retirement. Because individuals do not tend to save for their old age, institutions, including the federal government, have established mandatory pension plans.[14] These plans not only require persons to save for retirement, but in the instances where a mandatory retirement age is set, they define the time period during which an annuity must be accumulated.

The expressed desire of many college professors to continue working has caused some persons to suggest that retirement at any age may force out workers who have a contribution to make. The evidence about the correlation between age and productivity is equivocal.[15] Both positive and negative relations can be found,[16] and differences vary by field.[17] In some fields—history and philosophy, for example—great productivity occurs in the older years, but much of this productivity may be due to help from assistants and the aging professors' methods of work.[18] One study found that scientists produce more than their proportionate share of high-quality research before age 39.[19] Nevertheless, researchers have had little success finding an equation that describes the relation between productivity and age. Bayer and Dutton examined the relation between age and career performance of academic scientists. Discovering that no one model fit all disciplinary fields, they concluded that career age is a poor predictor of research and other professional activity.[20] However, Bayer and Dutton found that during the next decade a group of relatively less productive or eminent scientists will be moving into the age of retirement eligibility.

Various arguments have been made for permitting the able, motivated worker to continue. The American Medical Association opposes mandatory retirement, claiming that the sudden cessation of work and the loss of earning power can lead to serious physical and emotional deterioration for retirees, even early death.[21] The American public tends to favor the abolition of mandatory retirement. In response to a Harris Poll, 86% of the public agreed that workers who wanted to continue should not be forced to retire because of age. On the other hand, 49% of the respondents felt that a mandatory retirement age made sense because most people are ready to retire at age 65, and it is hard to make exceptions for those not ready.[22]

The delegates to the 1971 White House Conference on Aging recommended that chronological age *not* be the sole criterion for retirement; that employment possibilities beyond age 65 be made available; but also that realistic opportunities for retirement before age 65 be provided, including gradual and trial retirements.[23] The argument for abandoning the chronological age criterion has also been made on the basis that intellectual performance tends to remain high until shortly before death. Arguing that persons still engaged in intellectual growth should not be forced to retire, K. Warner Schaie also notes that "those who are on the downgrade early in life should not be required to contribute what they can no longer provide."[24]

Society's work patterns do seem destined to change. Alternative plans allowing persons past 50 to take sabbaticals, shorter work weeks, and gradual retirement, have been proposed.[25] And it is reasonable to assume that the quick growth of technology, accompanied by the rapid obsolescence of work skills, may require workers to undertake new jobs several times during their careers.[26] Professors may join other middle-aged and older workers in job retraining, long work sabbaticals, and periods of unemployment between jobs.

Whether raising the mandatory retirement age will have serious consequences for American colleges and universities obviously depends on how many academics decide to take advantage of the option. As will be discussed in chapter 2, the average mandatory retirement age in American colleges and universities is higher than in American business and industry. Furthermore, many academics retire before the mandatory age, and thus one might argue that raising the mandatory retirement age would have little effect.

A recent survey of American academics provides some idea of how faculty members might respond to an increase in the mandatory retirement age. Fifteen percent of the respondents reported that they plan to retire after age 65, and only 7% planned to work until age 70.[27] Initially, these results suggest that an increase in the mandatory retirement age would have little impact. However, as Ladd, Lipset, and Palmer point out, these persons were probably responding to the current retirement norm. When the responses are analyzed for institutions with higher mandatory retirement ages, respondents cited an older age at which they planned to retire. Furthermore, respondents closer to the retirement age tended to report plans to retire at older ages. This finding suggests that were the mandatory retirement age boosted substantially or removed entirely, there might be a gradual increase in the average retirement age in academia. If this is the case, colleges and universities may have even more reason to examine ways to induce faculty members to switch careers or retire early.

AN OVERVIEW OF CAREER OPTIONS

Alternative ways to encourage faculty members to make a career change or retire early are discussed in the following chapter. As yet, few institutions have implemented programs to facilitate mid-career change among their faculty members, but two types of related programs are available. The first is comprised of internship and fellowship programs which sometimes lead to mid-career change, although this is not their objective. The second type includes programs that retrain faculty members for other disciplines or specialties. Because there has been so little experience with mid-career change programs in academia, or even in industry, most of this book is devoted to early-retirement alternatives.

Unlike mid-career options, the range of special incentive early-retirement schemes seems unlimited. We selected the following ten variations for detailed analysis because they illustrate the range of basic options available.

Alternative 1: Full-Salary Early Annuity. Under this alternative, an organization pays a steep price to get some of its employees to retire early. During the period between an employee's early retirement and his mandatory retirement date, the organization pays him a supplement to the regular early-retirement benefits which brings his total retirement income to the level of his full (or nearly full) salary. Also, by purchasing a supplemental annuity to take effect on the mandatory retirement date, the organization assures the individual a future retirement income at least equal to what he would have recieved had he remained employed until the mandatory age.

Alternative 2: Severance Payment. An organization makes a limited, direct cash payment to an employee who leaves the organization before his mandatory retirement date. This settlement, which might be a multiple of the employee's annual salary, may be paid in a lump sum or over one year. The employee might also receive an early retirement pension if he is eligible for one under the standard retirement plan.

Alternative 3: Individual-Based Early Annuity.   Under this alternative, employees who retire early receive benefits comparable to those they would have received had they retired at the mandatory retirement age and had they received normal (or nearly normal) salary advancements until that age. To accomplish this, the organization supplements the individual's regular early-retirement benefits with direct payments. The organization also purchases a supplemental annuity to take effect at the mandatory retirement date, after which the direct payments cease. The difference between this alternative and Alternative 1 is that here the early-retirement income is equal to the projected mandatory retirement benefits, not the individual's pre-retirement salary.

Alternative 4: Group-Based Early Annuity.   Assuming that the more highly paid employees within a group of individuals of the same age and years of service are more highly valued, a group-based early annuity might be reasonable. This plan is similar to the individual-based early annuity, except that the supplemental benefits it provides both before and after mandatory retirement age are established in relation to the median projected mandatory-age benefits of all employees in the same age-service group. Those below the median receive a relatively larger supplement than those above it. Therefore, the incentive for them to retire is greater than for the higher-paid employees, whom the organization might prefer to retain.

Alternative 5: Individual-Based Early Annuity with Partial Employment.   As with the individual-based early annuity, the individual is assured a retirement income after the mandatory retirement age equal to what he would have received had he not retired early. Again, the organization purchases a supplemental annuity to take effect on the mandatory retirement date. But during the period between early and mandatory retirement, the retiree is retained in a part-time position which supplements his early-retirement benefits. There might be an upper limit on compensated employment, say 33% or 49%, of full-time work.

Alternative 6: Group-Based Early Annuity with Partial Employment.   This scheme also pairs part-time employment before the mandatory retirement age with supplemental benefits after that age. However, following the logic underlying Alternative 4, both the supplemental employment and the supplemental benefits are calculated in relation to the median projected mandatory-age benefits for one's age-service group. Extending this logic even further, this alternative could be modified to provide supplemental employment only to those employees whose salaries are above the median, under the assumption that they are the employees the organization would most like to retain in a productive capacity.

Alternative 7: Continued Annuity Contributions. An organization may continue payment into the annuity fund, or otherwise supplement the future annuity of an employee who retires early. Such payment is continued to the mandatory retirement age. Note that under this option the early retiree defers *all* retirement benefits until he reaches the mandatory retirement age.

Alternative 8: Severance Payment with Continued Annuity Contribution. This option is similar to Alternative 7; but, in addition to the continued annuity payments, the early retiree is provided a severance payment. Thus, this option is more like an early-retirement scheme since the employee may not need to find another job.

Alternative 9: Liberalized Benefits Schedule. Under this scheme, the normal benefits schedule for persons electing early retirement would be liberalized, typically through an across-the-board increase of all benefit rates.[28]

Alternative 10: Continued Perquisites. Employees retiring early under this alternative would not forfeit certain perquisites—for example, the use of an office, secretarial services, photocopying services, health services, and membership in group health and life insurance plans. If not used in conjunction with other options, this plan seems unlikely to become very popular.

THE VARIOUS PURPOSES OF EARLY RETIREMENT

Realistically, early retirement cannot solve all of academia's problems. It is only one of many remedies one can prescribe for the steady-state university. It should also be clear that early retirement is basically a short-term solution, one that would have to be applied in combination with other policies. As later chapters reveal, the major benefit of early retirement might not be financial savings but rather the release of "indentured labor." It could free disaffected faculty members who would be happier outside of the university but who remain because of financial need.

Early retirement, then, must be examined from several perspectives since it might be used to address several problems. It can be viewed as an academic policy, a move intended to open faculty ranks to new persons with needed skills. In this vein it could be used by a chancellor, dean, or other administrator to shift resources to needed areas, to new or expanding fields, or to programs that need rebuilding. By encouraging the early retirement of academics in crowded or out-of-demand fields, the administrator could gain a few faculty positions to reallocate elsewhere. However, the ability to shift resources to new areas is not always at hand.

Early retirement might also be seen as a fiscal policy. When viewed as an academic policy to move existing resources to a new area, early retirement does not change the school's total number of faculty members. But in a case where an institution is faced with a budgetary shortage and can continue to function with a reduced staff, early retirement might be a way to reduce payroll costs. Obviously this policy cannot be used extensively; a staff can be reduced in size only so much.

Early retirement might also be seen as part of an employee benefit package. Since most institutions have early-retirement schemes that permit persons who retire before the mandatory retirement age to draw a retirement annuity (one less, of course, than would be received at the mandatory retirement age), an increased-benefits early-retirement plan might be seen as another type of employee benefit.

Providing an increased-benefits retirement plan to most or all employees would be an expensive endeavor. An institution might conceivably publicize an increased-benefits early-retirement scheme as a benefits program while using it as a management tool. However, such a plan would appear to be a weak addition to a benefits package because retirement is not a salient issue to most individuals. The plan would have to be heavily promoted to be effective.

If an institution entices individuals to retire early and thus increases the retirement rate in the near-term, it may eventually experience a decrease in the retirement rate as it runs out of persons to retire early. Maintaining the inducements to early retirement could then become an expensive proposition. This observation does not suggest that an early-retirement policy is necessarily bad. An institution that needs more retirements now might be willing to accept fewer retirements in the future. In other institutions, the faculty may be so young that few positions are being freed by retirements. Thus, convincing some persons to retire early may have more positive than negative consequences. Retirement policy, of course, can be evaluated only by examining the specific age distribution for a college or university.

Increased interest in early retirement might cause academics to view it inaccurately as only an escape for the incompetent. Although some persons who desire early retirement have declined in productivity, not all have done so. Some highly productive employees retire early in order to pursue other activities while they still have the vigor. Stigmatizing early retirement would discourage such persons from retiring and would be unhealthy for both individuals and institutions. Academics should be free to terminate when they desire, and institutions should not be burdened by persons forced to remain because of peer pressure or financial necessity.

NOTES

1. A succinct definition of "steady-state" is next to impossible because the term has taken on such varied meanings, many quite different from an economist's definition, and others that are simply inaccurate. For a critique of the misinterpretations, see Lyman A. Glenny, "The Illusions of Steady State," *Change* 6, no. 10 (December/January 1974–75): 24–28. The use of the term, as it applies to colleges and universities, should be clear from the text. A comprehensive discussion of the concept of steady-state can be found in Herman E. Daly, ed., *Toward a Steady-State Economy* (San Francisco: W. H. Freeman and Company, 1973). For a discussion of the steady-state in higher education, see John G. Kemeny, "The University in Steady State," *Daedalus* 104, no. 1 (Winter 1975): 87–96. In regard to staffing problems see W. Todd Furniss, *Steady-State Staffing in Tenure-Granting Institutions, and Related Papers* (Washington, D.C.: American Council on Education, 1973). The steady-state condition is perhaps at its worst in Great Britain. See Harold Perkin, "The Financial Crisis in British Universities: Or How to Live with 29 Percent Inflation," *AAUP Bulletin* 61, no. 4 (December 1975): 304–308.

2. For a discussion of the effect of low growth on affirmative action, see Martin Trow, "The Implications of Low Growth Rates for Higher Education," mimeo. (Berkeley: University of California, Graduate School of Public Policy, June 1975): 14.

3. For an overview see Carnegie Foundation for the Advancement of Teaching, *More Than Survival: Prospects for Higher Education in a Period of Uncertainty* (San Francisco: Jossey-Bass, 1975) and Walter Adams, "The State of Higher Education: Myths and Realities," *AAUP Bulletin* 60, no. 2 (June 1974): 119–125.

4. Enrollment predictions for the 1970s were off as much as 10%. Guesses about enrollments for the 1980s are even more uncertain. Although most forecasters see a gradual increase in enrollments in the near future, the growth rate will certainly be less than in the 1960s. Future enrollments will depend on demographic factors, which can be predicted with some accuracy, and college attendance rates, which have been difficult to predict but which will be even more difficult to predict in the future when a greater percentage of the college population is composed of older persons and part-time students. Even if these numbers were known, projections would have to consider the capacity of the economy to absorb these college-educated persons. Stephen P. Dresch, "Educational Saturation: A Demographic-Economic Model," *AAUP Bulletin* 61, no. 3 (October 1975): 239–247. For a variety of enrollment projections, see: Carnegie Foundation, *More Than Survival,* especially Appendix B, pp. 141–147; Carnegie Commission on Higher Education, *Priorities for Action: Final Report of the Carnegie Commission on Higher Education* (New York: McGraw-Hill, 1973), pp. 95–106; Richard Berendzen, "Population Changes and Higher Education," *Educational Record* 55, no. 2 (Spring 1974): 115–125; and U.S. Department of Health, Education and Welfare, *Projections of Educational Statistics to 1982–1983* (Washington, D.C.: U.S. Government Printing Office, 1974), p. 24.

5. The demand for new doctorates has been steadily declining and may disappear within the next decade. See Roy Radner and Leonard S. Miller, *Demand and Supply in U.S. Higher Education* (New York: McGraw-Hill, 1975). The director of the National Science Foundation has argued that this decline may have serious implications for science research in America. See Richard C. Atkinson, "The Threat to Scientific Research, " *Chronicle of Higher Education*, 28 March 1977, p. 40.

6. Some nontraditional or extended degree programs have been established in part to capture a new clientele. Although few colleges and universities tried to recruit adults during the last ten years, most plan to do so during the next decade. See Carnegie Foundation, *More than Survival*, pp. 96–100. Several universities launched extended degree programs in response to anticipated declining enrollments; see Carl Vernon Patton, "Extended Education in an Elite Institution: Are There Sufficient Incentives to Encourage Faculty Participation?" *Journal of Higher Education* 46, no. 4 (July/August 1975):

427–444; and Leland Medsker, Stewart Edelstein, Hannah Kreplin, Janet Ruyle, and John Shea, *Extending Opportunities for a College Degree: Practice, Problems and Potentials* (Berkeley: University of California, Center for Research and Development in Higher Education, 1975).

7. Carnegie Foundation, *More than Survival*, pp. 82–85.

8. Patton, "Extended Education."

9. Abolishing tenure, even when institutions are faced with deficits, cannot be done overnight. Determining what makes a financial exigency may be difficult, and faculty rights and contractual agreements certainly must be recognized. For a landmark case involving the abolition of tenure and the laying-off of tenured employees because of financial difficulties, see "The Bloomfield College Case," *AAUP Bulletin* 60, no. 3 (September 1974): 320–330. The court ordered the terminated employees reinstated. Its decision was upheld on first appeal, and the college apparently will not appeal again: "Bloomfield Decision Upheld," *Academe* 9, no. 4 (December 1975): 1, 3. The AAUP has recognized that appointments can be terminated because of a "demonstrably *bona fide* financial exigency." See "Termination of Faculty Appointments because of Financial Exigency, Discontinuance of a Program or Department or for Medical Reasons," *AAUP Bulletin* 60, no. 4 (December 1974): 411–413.

10. Allan M. Cartter and John M. McDowell, "Projecting Market and Institutional Policy Impact on Faculty Composition," mimeo. (Los Angeles: University of California, Department of Higher Education, February 1975).

11. How the elimination of tenure would affect the quality of education has not been determined. Most institutions have some form of tenure, which may still be needed to protect academic freedom. The issue certainly cannot be settled here. See Bardwell L. Smith, ed., *The Tenure Debate* (San Francisco: Jossey-Bass, 1973); and Commission on Academic Tenure in Higher Education, *Faculty Tenure* (San Francisco: Jossey-Bass, 1973).

12. Public Law 95-256 [H.R. 5383], Age Discrimination in Employment Act Amendments of 1978; April 6, 1978.

13. "AAUP Opposed to Exemption of Tenured Professors," *Academe* 11, no. 4 (December 1977): 1.

14. Juanita M. Kreps, "Economics of Aging," in Ethel Shanas, ed., *Aging in Contemporary Society* (Beverly Hills, California: Sage Publications, 1970), p. 86. This seems to be the case in Great Britain as well. See Dorothy Wedderburn, "Old People in Britain," in Shanas, ed., *Aging in Contemporary Society*, p. 101. The delegates to the 1971 White House Conference on Aging recognized this problem. "Too many individuals fail to plan for retirement or plan too late." 1971 White House Conference on Aging, *Sec-*

tion Recommendations on Employment and Retirement (Washington, D.C.: U.S. Government Printing Office, 1971), p. 6.

15. Frank Clemente, "Early Career Determinants of Research Productivity," *American Journal of Sociology* 79, no. 2 (September 1973): 409–419; and Donald C. Pelz and Frank M. Andrews, *Scientists in Organizations* (New York: John Wiley, 1966).

16. James L. Bess, "Integrating Faculty and Student Life Cycles," *Review of Educational Research* 43, no. 4 (Fall 1973): 377–403.

17. Harvey C. Lehman, *Age and Achievement* (Princeton, New Jersey: Princeton University Press, 1953).

18. Wayne Dennis, "Creative Productivity Between the Ages of 20 and 80," in Bernice L. Neugarten, ed., *Middle Age and Aging* (Chicago: University of Chicago Press, 1968), pp. 106–114.

19. Harvey C. Lehman, "The Creative Production Rates of Present Versus Past Generations of Scientists," in Neugarten, ed., *Middle Age and Aging*, pp. 104–105. A longitudinal study of fifty-three scientists suggests that productivity does not decline with age among *eminent* research scientists. See Anne Roe, "Changes in Scientific Activities with Age," *Science* 150, no. 3694 (October 1965): 313–318.

20. Alan E. Bayer and Jeffrey E. Dutton, "Career Age and Research-Professional Activities of Academic Scientists," paper presented at the annual meeting of the American Educational Research Association (Washington, D.C.: April 1975).

21. American Medical Association, Committee on Aging, *Retirement: A Medical Philosophy and Approach* (Chicago: AMA, 1972). But see Suzanne G. Haynes, Anthony J. McMichael and Herman A. Tyroler, "Survival After Early and Normal Retirement," *Journal of Gerontology* 33, no. 2 (March 1978): pp. 269–278.

22. Louis Harris and Associates, *The Myth and Reality of Aging in America* (Washington, D.C.: National Council on the Aging, 1975), p. 214.

23. White House Conference on Aging, *Section Recommendations on Employment and Retirement* (Washington, D.C.: U.S. Government Printing Office, 1971), pp. 4, 9.

24. K. Warner Schaie, "Translations in Gerontology—From Lab to Life: Intellectual Functioning," *American Psychologist* 29, no. 11 (November 1974): p. 806.

25. Juanita M. Kreps, "Career Options After Fifty: Suggested Research," *The Gerontologist* 11, no. 1 (Spring 1971): pp. 4–8.

26. Bernice L. Neugarten, "The Old and the Young in Modern Societies," in Shanas, ed., *Aging in Contemporary Society*, p. 18.

27. Everett Carll Ladd, Jr., Seymour Martin Lipset, and David D. Palmer, "The American Professoriate: The Issue of Mandatory Retirement," mimeo. (Storrs, Conn., School of Business Administration: 1977). Summarized as Everett Carll Ladd, Jr., and Seymour Martin Lipset, "Many Professors Would Postpone Retirement if Law Were Changed (The Ladd-Lipset Faculty Survey)," *Chronicle of Higher Education*, 7 November 1977, pp. 7–8.

28. Across-the-board increases in early-retirement benefits would be expensive. Providing an unreduced formula benefit at age 60 rather than at 65 would increase the employer's retirement cost by approximately 50%. Providing normal benefits at 55 rather than 65 would increase the cost by almost 100%. See William C. Greenough and Francis P. King, "Is Normal Retirement at Age 65 Obsolete?" *Pension World* 13, no. 6 (June 1977): 35–36.

2

Career Options in Industry, Government, and Academia

In efforts to cut costs and encourage faculty turnover, some colleges and universities have initiated increased-benefits early-faculty retirement plans. More than two dozen institutions have early-retirement schemes that provide in certain circumstances a supplement for income lost because of early retirement.[1] A few institutions have also tried mid-career change programs or have made other attempts to encourage faculty members to retrain so that they can shift to areas more in demand. In devising these schemes, academia has had the opportunity to examine similar attempts by industry. Industry has apparently had success with incentive early retirement, but its experience with mid-career change has been limited. Although many businesses and industries regularly offer in-service training, these programs are typically intended to improve an employee's performance in his current position.

During interviews with executives, we found minimal interest in mid-career change programs. From the viewpoint of an individual enterprise, there is little reason to retrain an employee for another profession, especially when there are easier, more direct ways to eliminate unneeded employees. Yet there have been several attempts to establish career-change programs in industry, government, and academia.

Now that the golden days are behind us and competition for employment is severe both in and out of the academic world, a great deal of attention is being directed at the issues of career development and career change.[2] Career change is not new. Anyone leaving a job before the normal retirement age is involved in career change. Even during the growth period of higher education, some academics decided to change careers, and a portion of those who did not attain tenure chose to leave academic life rather than take a position in a different university. The bulk of career change in academia clearly has been among faculty members who failed to obtain tenure. Even much of the recent interest has involved consideration of options for untenured faculty members.

A recent booklet by *Change* magazine outlines career alternatives for academics, but it addresses primarily nontenured faculty members and administrators.[3] Universities and colleges may also need programs to stimulate and facilitate career change among persons who cannot be forced to move to another career by the threat of unemployment. Unfortunately, the literature on career change contains little information on programs relevant to academics. In one study of mid-life career redirection, most of the programs described pertain only to blue-collar and lower-level white-collar occupations.[4] The programs most relevant to academics are those aimed at assisting out-of-work aerospace engineers and scientists. However, these programs failed as vehicles for career change and reemployment, although information services which directed individuals to alternative job opportunities were somewhat effective.[5]

MID-CAREER CHANGE IN INDUSTRY

Private industry's experience with career retraining has been well documented in the volumes cited above.[6] We attempted to cover the terrain once more, but with exclusive attention to the retraining of highly educated, high-level technical or managerial personnel—persons who occupy positions that could be considered comparable to those held by faculty members in academia. We did not discover any career-retraining programs for persons at this level. Other researchers have also failed to find such programs.[7]

It appears that there is little incentive for industry to retrain persons who have attained relatively high positions in a firm. If they become superfluous through obsolescence of their knowledge or the erosion of their creativity and energy, they are dealt with in more traditional ways: termination or early retirement. If a firm is well-off or has a "full-employment" policy, they may be moved to a less responsible position or assigned a special task until they are eligible for regular or early retirement.

This is not to say that industry lacks training programs for highly placed personnel. On the contrary, some firms, especially in high-technology industries, have extensive programs, both in-house and at universities. But these programs are invariably upgrading programs through which highly valued employees are made conversant with state-of-the-art developments in their own or in related fields in order to ensure their continued value to the firm.

MID-CAREER CHANGE IN THE FEDERAL GOVERNMENT

A lack of mid-career retraining programs is also found in the federal government. Even in the military, where the careers of both enlisted men and officers may end at relatively young ages, there is no mid-career change program. Although the military does not now conduct an organized pre-retirement counseling service, there once was an official program. It was discontinued in 1974 because the Government Accounting Office concluded that such a service was not properly a function of the military. That program had two parts: (1) Project Referral, a computer-based résumé referral system; and (2) Project Transition, a counseling service in the base organization which advised potential retirees and worked with private industry and federally supported on-the-job training programs. The military service now holds pre-retirement briefing sessions. During these meetings, retirement pay is explained, and usually some attempt is made to offer suggestions about establishing a second career.[8]

The Retired Officers Association offers an employment service for its members from all branches of the armed forces. The Association conducts a national résumé referral service. It also offers two booklets: one gives advice about career planning, and the other is a practical guide for establishing a second career.

A program which formally combines early retirement with career retraining exists for air traffic controllers employed by the Federal Aviation Administration. Because of the stressful nature of their work and the extreme consequences of their errors, the law provides for their removal for "operational or medical" reasons and for retirement at age 56. The law also provides for retraining for a second career (generally expected to be in government services), with up to two years of full-time training at full pay and reimbursement of educational expenses.[9] Since this program is relatively new, there is not a great deal of experience with the placement of retrainees. However, one observer claims that the placement record has been poor.[10]

MID-CAREER CHANGE IN ACADEMIA

We expected to find few formal career retraining programs for academics. We reasoned that institutions have little incentive to become involved in retraining junior faculty members, whose contracts they could merely not renew, or tenured faculty members, few of whom could be expected to give up secure positions in a contracting job market. Furthermore, a substantial minority of academics has always moved easily between academic and nonacademic settings. Industry, government, philanthropic institutions, and nonacademic research organizations regularly hire academics and lose some of their employees to colleges and universities. Those who make these moves either require no retraining because they already possess the skills for operating in the new environment, or they are sufficiently sophisticated about educational opportunities to acquire new skills without third-party intervention. Although we failed to locate any programs directed at the retraining of tenured faculty members for different substantive areas of new work situations, our search did reveal two types of programs relevant to our interests: (1) internship and fellowship programs which sometimes lead to career changes, and (2) programs which retrain faculty members for work in a different academic specialty or discipline.

Internship and Fellowship Programs

Programs such as the Economic Policy Fellowships of the Brookings Institution and the Congressional Science and Engineering Fellowships of the American Association for the Advancement of Science (AAAS) offer opportunities for professors to experiment with new kinds of work in new settings.[11] Although the programs are seldom directed toward career change—their overt goals are the enrichment of the professor's experience and capabilities or those of the host organization—a substantial minority of recipients remain with the host organization or with similar organizations outside the academic world. For example, among approximately thirty academics who participated in the Congressional Science and Engineering Fellowship program of the AAAS during the academic years 1973-74, 1974-75, and 1975-76, almost half remained in nonacademic, public policy positions.

Since these programs are generally administered by outside agencies, colleges and universities have little control over the selection of grantees. It is possible that the selection criteria used by funders and host agencies will be counterproductive from the perspective of an institution which would like to encourage career change. The former may select the most creative and promising candidates, while the latter would like to encourage career change among the least productive. If this is so, then only institutions interested in encouraging gross turnover among faculty members should find these programs attractive. On the other hand, it is possible that the creative people who elect to stay on in new jobs would no longer be of as much value to their former academic departments because of the change in their interests. In either case, it is unlikely that internships and fellowship programs would be of much help to institutions that want to encourage career change among their least-valued faculty members.

Retraining Programs

The desire to reduce or abolish selected academic programs while maintaining employment commitments to faculty members has caused several institutions, including the State University System of Florida, the Pennsylvania State Colleges, the State University of New York, and the University of Wisconsin, to establish retraining programs. Although they are not precisely on career-change programs because the professors continue in the same institution or system, such retraining programs do give institutions the flexibility to reallocate resources to more productive use.

Recognizing the declining rate growth of student enrollments in the Florida State University System, the Florida Board of Regents authorized funds for faculty development or retraining. The funds were intended to aid *tenured* faculty members in departments with declining enrollments to retrain themselves in an area in which faculty manpower is needed. The $3,000 retraining grants were made available within the State University System to pay the costs of a retrainee's relocation, tuition, and other expenses associated with graduate study. The grantees, selected by campus-wide screening committees, were released from instruction and research for two to four quarters. During the retraining period the faculty member continued to receive his full salary. He agreed to return to his university to teach for at least one year, or to repay the University System one-half of his salary and the full amount of the grant. In return, the university agreed to find him an appropriate tenured appointment. In selected cases the retrainee's institution was provided funds to help pay for a replacement faculty member, and in other cases retraining could have been part-time and spread over more than one academic year. The program operated from 1974 until 1977.

The Pennsylvania State Colleges program operates similarly, but has several differences. The program is *not* limited to tenured faculty members, and the retrained faculty member is assured reassignment within the same institution. In the Florida program, the retrainee could be reassigned to another institution in the system. Furthermore, the funds for expenses other than the retrainee's regular salary are administered by a separate entity, the Pennsylvania State College Educational Services Trust. This program begun in 1975, is still operating but at a reduced scale.

In 1977 the State University of New York (SUNY) adopted faculty retraining as one way to deal with possible layoffs. A program was devised to permit tenured faculty members to retrain in fields more in demand. Candidates are nominated to the central administration and are selected upon recommendation of an advisory committee. The faculty member typically spends a semester in retraining, usually at a state university. He receives his salary, partial support for books and travel, and a tuition waiver if he studies in the SUNY system.

The Wisconsin program was launched in 1974 when the University was threatened by possible retrenchment. The program has varied in content and in the number of persons enrolled. Initially decisions were made on a person-by-person basis by individual campuses. Now recommendations are made by the campuses and selections are made on a system-wide basis. Provided salary and tuition, the trainee usually studies for two semesters in an in-state institution.

During the field stage of our project only the Florida and Pennsylvania programs were truly in operation. The Wisconsin program had one person engaged in retraining, and the SUNY program had not yet begun. A recent paper indicates that the Wisconsin and SUNY programs are similar in form and content to the Florida and Pennsylvania programs.[12] Our analysis of the latter two programs revealed a number of issues important both to institutions which might enact similar programs and to individuals who would participate in them.

Financing.   Very little new funding is involved because the major costs are the retrainees' salaries, which continue to be paid out of regular budget lines. This appears to be a straightforward solution to the funding problem, but it raises other issues that may affect the willingness of campuses, schools, and departments to participate in the program with their own resources. On the other hand, if a position is slated for elimination, there is little loss in temporarily allocating the budget line to retraining. Indeed, there may be a net gain in morale among faculty members within the affected department.

Content of the Retraining Program.   Retraining in these programs varies from preparation in an allied speciality within the same discipline to training for an entirely new, unrelated discipline. In some cases advanced degrees are earned, but this is not always a program goal. The content of the retraining program is worked out on an ad hoc basis for each participant. In one instance, the receiving department, with the consent of the retrainee, enlisted a faculty member from the same discipline at a respected neighboring institution to help design the retraining program and to act as a mediator between the retrained professor and the receiving department. The arrangement apparently worked well.

Application and Decision Process.   Both programs began with a centralized application and screening procedure and now rely on a decentralized system of campus-based initial screening. In each case, participating units perceive a benefit in retaining some degree of local autonomy in the selection of participants. Nevertheless, the prerogative of a central authority to allocate resources and approve lower-level decisions has been retained in both programs.

Under some circumstances, interest in the retraining program depends on one's position in the system. For example, a department may be indifferent to retraining decisions if it is slated to lose positions in any case. An institution within a system may be opposed to retraining if it operates with a fixed faculty allocation and if participation in retraining means having some faculty members on leave with pay. The system's central office may favor the retraining because the additional costs are small and the prospect of increased future productivity is attractive.

The programs formally receive applications on the initiative of interested individuals, but third parties often begin the process by encouraging particular individuals to apply. This "encouragement" sometimes has consisted of notice that one's position was to be abolished. Many of the Pennsylvania State Colleges' participants became involved in this way; and, although the "retrenchment" of their positions was eventually retracted, many continued in their plans to retrain.

Placement. Placement is rarely a separate process. Generally, candidates for retraining are selected only if a new placement has already been negotiated for them. Sometimes, though, details about joint appointments, courses to be taught, seniority, etc., remain to be decided even after the major decisions about retraining and placement have been made. These are potential trouble spots. When a person may join a department only with its consent as is true in most academic institutions some mechanism for negotiating transfers of faculty members needs to be worked out. In these two programs, the transfers seem to have been arranged on an ad hoc basis.

The Pennsylvania State Colleges program encountered some special difficulties due to the existence of both *tenure* and *seniority.* The parties to the collective bargaining agreement disagreed about the meaning of these provisions. Some maintained that they are identical, while others asserted that tenure adheres to a faculty member's position within the institution and seniority adheres to the individual within his department. Such issues raise the specter of conflict between the interests of the re-trainee and those of other members of the receiving department. We found that in some instances the matter was so difficult to resolve that the retrained faculty member remained formally in his old department while serving full- or part-time in the new department, each department being compensated in proportion to the professor's level of effort.

Any institution considering such retraining programs must be sensitive to similar complications arising out of its own contractual arrangements with faculty members or with faculty bargaining agents. One should also expect to encounter early difficulties stemming from the disciplinary and departmental modes of academic organization that are generally not receptive to individuals crossing lines in mid-career. Support, on the other hand, is likely to come from the increased acceptance of faculty development as a legitimate activity of academics and their institutions.[13]

Career-change programs are appealing in concept, but the overriding question is whether any institution has the incentive to pay for these efforts. Business and industry see little benefit in financing programs which would retrain workers for employment elsewhere. The federal government has seen fit not to offer these programs to civil service or military employees. At least four universities have launched career-change programs, but they are basically internal programs; the retrained professor continues to work within his former institution. Where would institutions obtain the funds to support programs that would retrain faculty members for careers in business and industry? It seems unlikely that colleges and universities would use their own resources for this purpose. One proposal would have the federal government subsidize the retraining of workers through the unemployment compensation system.[14] Dr. Richard Atkinson, director of the National Science Foundation, has suggested that the government might facilitate mid-career change by subsidizing university retirement plans or by instituting a grant program. He sees the grant program allowing mid-career professors to remain on the faculty to conduct research while freeing that faculty member's salary to hire a younger person who would teach as well as conduct research. Dr. Atkinson has also suggested using tax incentives to encourage the formation of institutes where middle-aged scientists who leave teaching would devote all their time to research.[15]

Finding ways to cause academics to retrain in mid-career will be a formidable task. The early experimenters found that it is difficult to attract faculty members to retraining programs; the arrangements may be difficult to finance; and there may be status problems. For older faculty members, early retirement might be more appropriate. Industry's experience with schemes to encourage employees to retire early is instructive.

EARLY RETIREMENT IN INDUSTRY

Industry has found a number of ways to reduce the work force and to weed out marginal performers.[16] Lump-sum severance payments, supplements to both private pensions and social security, and other perquisites have been provided, all intended to cause certain employees to retire early.

Today, 96% of the pension plans in industry provide for early retirement. Most plans require an early retiree to take the actuarially reduced value of his accrued benefits, the reduction reflecting both the smaller amount contributed to the pension fund and the increased time during which the benefits will be paid. In 22% of the plans, however, liberalized benefits are provided to persons who voluntarily retire early.[17] These increased benefits are provided in several ways:

1. A liberalized early-retirement discount may be offered. The accrued retirement benefit is still reduced for each year the employee is under the mandatory retirement age, but the reduction is not as severe as the standard actuarial reduction.

2. The full benefit that would be received at the mandatory retirement age may be given without any reduction for early retirement.

3. The regular early-retirement benefit may be supplemented until the early retiree reaches age 65, when he can draw an unreduced social-security benefit.

These benefits may be *general,* in that they apply to all employees who meet the eligibility requirements for early retirement. On the other hand, they may be *senior supplements,* restricted to a class of employees who meet more stringent age and service requirements. Or they may be *company-option supplements,* applicable only to employees the company asks to retire. The general and senior supplements have grown in use during the last decade, while the company-option supplement is mainly limited to a few specific industries.[18] Recent changes in the Age Discrimination in Employment Act affect the way in which the company option can be administered since employees cannot be involuntarily retired before age 70 simply because of their age.

In order to obtain current information useful to colleges and universities considering early-retirement options, we interviewed selected firms included in a previous study of early retirement in business and industry[19] as well as a number of other firms with recent experience. We found that "early retirement" is often another name for termination, and termination programs generally apply to a wide range to employees. In some cases early-retirement programs apply to selected groups—usually high-level managers and professionals. Except in a few firms, modest numbers of persons have retired under these options.

The early retirement or termination programs fall into the following basic categories:

1. One-time payments, sometimes spread over a number of years.

2. Liberalization of the early-retirement actuarial reduction.

3. A pension supplement, sometimes geared to expected social-security income.

4. Part-time reemployment, often at a special task.

How do firms decide on the ingredients for their early-retirement schemes? How do they establish the benefit levels? We approached those firms whose early-retirement plans have successfully encouraged people to retire early. Although we cannot reveal the names of specific corporations, their experiences, summarized in Table 1, enable us to suggest alternatives useful to academia. Since the following information was collected before the 1978 amendments to the Age Discrimination in Employment Act, we should expect that modifications to some of these plans will be made in the near future.

Firm C1

This firm's formal early-retirement program is a permanent arrangement available at the employee's discretion. Employees who have reached age 58 with thirty years of service may retire early and receive a monthly pension, calculated like a normal pension but reduced one-half of one percent for each month between the retirement date and age 60. A person retiring after age 60 with thirty years of service does not receive an actuarial reduction. With more than ten but less than thirty years of service to his credit, a person age 60 receives a pension which is reduced one-third of one percent for each month before age 65 (mandatory retirement age). Any person retiring before age 62 receives a social-security supplement. This arrangement, negotiated by the union, is available to all employees.

In addition, this firm has an unpublicized scheme intended for management employees who "have gone stale" or who are "not able to cut it." If such a person is near the retirement age, the retirement options are pointed out to him. If it takes more to get him to retire, his manager may work out a "special" arrangement. Since this is a large firm, however, such problem employees can often be relocated.

Although this firm has not had extensive experience with induced early retirement, over 60% of its employees are retiring early, and most of the early retirees leave more than a year or two early. For example, in one typical month, 60% of all retirees left early, and only 15% of these retired just one or two years early.

Firm C2

Like most companies, Firm C2 has a retirement plan which includes a regular early-retirement provision. A person retiring before age 60 has his pension reduced 3% per year for each year he retires early. A person retiring at age 55 would receive a pension equal to 85% of his accrued annuity. The firm feels this arrangement encourages a reasonable turnover

Table 1 Selected Corporate Incentive Early Retirement Programs

Essence of Plan	Formal/ Informal	Temporary/ Permanent	Eligibility Requirements	Comments
C1. Liberalized actuarial discount. No actuarial discount if age 60, with 30 years of service. A social-security supplement is paid until early retiree begins to draw social security at age 62.	Formal	Permanent	Age 58, thirty years of service; Age 60, ten to thirty years of service	Special arrangements made for highly paid executives.
C2. Two years' salary paid monthly for up to four years or to age 65.	Formal	Temporary	Twenty-five years of service	Offered occasionally as need to reduce the size of the workforce arises.
C3. Half of regular salary plus a pension supplement to the balance of the salary paid till age 62.	Formal	Permanent	Age 60 to 62, ten years of service	Offered primarily to salespersons. Participant is placed on 50% salary and put on consultation. At age 62 can draw an unreduced annuity.
C4. Up to two years of salary paid over twelve months.	Informal	Permanent	Age 50 to 60, fifteen years of service	Used to remove marginal employees. Replaces a supplemental annuity option.
C5. Lump-sum payment of 50 to 100% of current salary.	Informal	Temporary	Age 55	Intended for executives, top management.

Essence of Plan	Formal/Informal	Temporary/Permanent	Eligibility Requirements	Comments
C6. One year's salary paid over two years or until age 65.	Informal	Permanent	Long service	Aimed at highly paid executives.
C7. An unreduced annuity plus $200 per month: at ages 55 to 59, till age 62; at ages 60 to 62, for 2 years; at ages 63 to 64, till age 65.	Formal	Temporary	Age 55, thirty years of service less two years for each year above 55	Used at all levels of employment. Many retired under this option.
C8. No actuarial discount.	Formal	Permanent	Age 62 or thirty years of service;	
Supplement from early retirement till age 62. Then, after the employee begins to draw social security, the supplement is reduced by about 50%.	Formal	Permanent	Age 60 and thirty years of service	Limited to hourly employees, clerical help, and managers. Intended as a supplement until recipient becomes eligible for social security.
C9. No actuarial discount plus 50% of social-security benefits to 65. Medical, life insurance continued.	Formal	Permanent	Age 62, thirty years of service	Available to all; 66% choose early retirement. Largest number in late fifties.
Liberalized actuarial discount plus 50% supplement to age 62. Life insurance continued.	Formal	Permanent	Age 55, ten years of service	

Essence of Plan	Formal/ Informal	Temporary/ Permanent	Eligibility Requirements	Comments
C10. Liberalized actuarial discount plus 50% of social-security benefits. Medical, life insurance continued.	Formal	Permanent	Age 55, fifteen years of service	Available to all; 55% choose early retirement. Necessary as a competitive benefit, but of course they hope to induce marginal performers to choose it.
C11. No actuarial discount. Modified medical, life insurance.	Formal	Permanent	Age plus years of service equal 85	Available to all, 50% choose early retirement, 66% hourly workers.
"Pre-retirement leave of absence": early-retirement benefits plus social-security equivalent to age 62.	Informal	Permanent	Age 57, fifteen years of service; salaried personnel	"Voluntary"—but initiated, approved, and packaged by management before employee is approached. Used to reduce division size and to remove marginal employees.
C12. Besides standard early retirement, there is "discretionary retirement." No actuarial discount plus a $250/month social-security supplement to age 62.	Informal	Permanent	Over 55, age plus service equal 80; salaried personnel	Used in plant closings. "Occasionally" for specific individuals.
C13. No actuarial discount.	Formal	Permanent	Age plus years of service equal 85.	Has existed for many years.
Liberalized actuarial discount.	Formal	Permanent	Age plus years of service less than 85; age 55 to 62	

Essence of Plan	Formal/ Informal	Temporary/ Permanent	Eligibility Requirements	Comments
C14. No actuarial discount.	Formal	Permanent	Age plus years of service equal 75.	Few people are taking this option. Only 25% of firm's retirements are early.
Liberalized actuarial discount.	Formal	Permanent	Age plus years of service less than 75; age 58 to 62	
C15. No actuarial discount.	Formal	Permanent	Age 62, twenty years of service	Available to all.
C16. No actuarial discount.	Formal	Permanent	Age 58, twenty-seven years of service	Available to all, hourly and salary. Most retire at age 62.
Liberalized actuarial discount.	Formal	Permanent	Age 50, ten years of service	
C17. No actuarial discount.	Formal	Permanent	Age 62 or age plus service equal 85	Eighty percent choose early retirement, mostly at age 62.
Liberalized actuarial discount. Modified medical, life insurance continued.	Formal	Permanent	Age 55	Available to all office personnel. Fifty percent choose it at various ages.
C18. Liberalized actuarial discount. Medical, life insurance continued.	Formal	Permanent	Age 55, ten years of service	Available to all.
Early-retirement plus lump-sum payment equal to "severance or a little more."	Informal	Unofficial	Age 55, ten years of service	"You *will* retire or be terminated." Only applied to non-union, salaried personnel.

among older employees. Management is not sure that it wants to provide "massive" incentives for early retirement.

During periods of severe manpower surpluses, this firm has offered a "special separation allowance" to anyone with twenty-five or more years of service. Most of the persons who took the option were at least 55 years of age. They received two years' pay spread over four years or until they reached age 65. This option has been offered twice, both times for limited periods. Another offering will be made soon to employees at a specific installation.

Firm C2 considers early retirement nonselective. If a person is not performing well, he is given job counseling rather than being encouraged to retire early. The special early-retirement provision is reserved for cases of excess labor supply. According to management, employee reaction to the special, temporary program has been highly favorable. The firm believes the option has saved it money, but it argues that it is difficult to track employee-replacement and associated costs.

A special separation payment was selected over higher lifetime benefits because it would be easier to keep the arrangement temporary. According to the firm, setting the level of the benefit involved a little magic. Considering existing early-retirement incomes, the supplement seemed enough. More would have seemed over-generous, perhaps wasteful. Two years' salary seemed right. Our informant believes that the firm would not have gotten a much higher acceptance rate if it had offered three years' pay instead of two.

Management considers the program well received. Out of a total of 160,000 employees, 8,000 were eligible. Below age 55, there was a 1% acceptance rate; for employees aged 55 to 59, the rate was 44%; and at ages 60 to 64, the rate was 75%. Acceptance rates did not vary by occupational category. Age was obviously the most important variable: over half of the persons qualifying with twenty-five years of service were below age 55, but only 1% of those persons took the option. (Note, however, that persons under age 55 were not eligible for a pension.)

Unlike the procedure in some other firms and universities, electing this early-retirement option was straightforward. The employee would submit a request for retirement to his manager, who would pass it along to personnel and the corporate headquarters. There the details were taken care of for the employee. Although the employee was asked to participate in an exit interview, the firm claims he did not have to negotiate a bureaucratic maze. He had elected the option, so there was no reason to impose company consent.

Firm C2 is generally satisfied with its experience with increased-benefits early retirement. It met the firm's needs, and management believes that as long as the option is flexible, it can work to the company's advantage. However, management did warn that the more often early retirement is encouraged, the more it affects retirement patterns in the future. Furthermore, early retirement may come to be seen as an employee benefit. Before offering the option again, therefore, this firm will ask whether it is worth the risk, especially in light of recent concerns about the discriminatory nature of these programs.

Firm C3

Firm C3's early retirement plan, which the firm says is more properly an "inactive-service" program, provides the early retiree with 50% of his salary plus money from consulting assignments. Offered only to certain workers, the option is not generally known to employees, nor is it mentioned in the firm's retirement booklet. It is aimed at salesmen aged 60 to 62 with ten years of service. (At age 62 an employee can retire with full pension.) Approximately seventy-five persons have accepted the company option.

The firm reports that some persons on the program are bitter. As our informant pointed out, this scheme is not really an "offer." Rather, it is a management decision, and employees take the option because the alternative is termination.

The company is now considering another type of inactive-service program. It intends to devise a program which will cause certain persons to leave early and make way for young persons. Already less than one-third of its retirees terminate at the mandatory age of 65. Most retire between 62 (when they may take an unreduced annuity) and 65. Very few now retire before 62, unless they are placed on the inactive-service program.

Firm C4

This large firm distinguishes between a person who retires after vesting (ten years of service required) and one who has fifteen years of service and has reached age 60. The latter person is designated as an annuitant and is provided additional benefits, such as a continuation of life insurance. If an employee retires voluntarily before age 60, his pension is not supplemented.

An early retirement at the company option is supplemented. When the company terminates a person early, a severance allowance is paid in accordance with a formula that differs for annuitants and others. Up to two years' salary may be paid in installments up to twelve months, as the employee desires. The exact payment depends upon the employee's age and the number of years of service credit.

This option has been used to eliminate surplus employees, ineffective performers, and satisfactory employees impeding the advancement of new, more effective employees. Employees in all three categories received the same treatment.

Although the firm uses this option to rid itself of poor performers, it encourages others to volunteer for the program. So far, management thinks it has been able to cause the "right" persons to take the option. In establishing the benefit levels, the firm tried to match what people would be getting under an old program which offered a supplemental annuity for life. Hospital insurance, family-income insurance, and product discounts are also provided.

The firm has not saved much money under this alternative because most people who have left early have had to be replaced. However, the company is satisfied that the option has succeeded in removing marginal employees.

Firm C5

This firm has an informal, temporary program which makes a severance payment to a person the firm wants to transfer but who would rather not leave the area. The payment is determined individually. The benefit formula, roughly related to years of service, provides about a year's pay, usually made in a lump sum. Life insurance to age 65, medical coverage, and a supplement to Medicare are provided along with the payment. The closer an early retiree is to age 65, the smaller the payment.

This firm has not relied solely on this scheme to solve its manpower problems. Like several other companies, it is large enough to handle many of its problems with transfers. When a person is identified as surplus, the firm's active job-placement program attempts to find a new position for him.

Special early retirees comprise a small fraction of the firm's annuitants. The firm has 20,000 employees on the retired roles, but only 75 left with incentive early retirements. Management is concerned that making pensions too generous may drain away the good people.

Firm C6

This firm has two plans. One is a normal severance-allowance program that is granted to individuals whose jobs have been eliminated because of technological advancements or for cost reduction. The amount varies, depending upon length of service and how close an employee is to retirement; it tapers off at age 62.

The second scheme is a special program which is administered by a committee that controls salaries for upper management. When a person is blocking organizational change, the company may grant a more generous severance allowance to move him out. When necessary, such persons are paid up to one year's pay over two years. The option exists to serve the needs of management. It is used selectively, and our informant stressed that there was no guarantee that an eligible employee would receive the option. In fact, only two or three employees per year are removed under this scheme. Like other larger firms, this business tries to relocate an employee before terminating him under the early-retirement scheme.

Firm C7

In 1971, Firm C7 looked to the future and saw a downturn in business. Hiring was reduced, business began to slack off, and the firm anticipated imminent layoffs. Upon examining employee age distributions, the firm saw it would not be able to hire young employees, upon whom it had depended in the past. Corporate management felt that if it could not hire, the firm would face stagnation. On the other hand, it did not want to fire established employees.

"Management was willing to spend a few dollars to enhance retirement for persons in older age groups," our informant told us. A plan was drawn up that would cause some employees to leave. By not refilling all the vacated spaces, management would reduce the work force while avoiding layoffs. Persons who met the criteria (age plus years of service totaling 85 at age 55, or one point less than 85 for each full year older than 55) were offered unreduced annuities plus $200 per month until age 62. Persons aged 60 to 62 at retirement would receive the $200 until age 65 (the mandatory retirement age).

Group life insurance was retained in full force until age 65, when it would begin to decrease to a lifetime minimum, and basic health-care protection and major medical were maintained for life. Individuals covered under the company's survivor-income plan or the survivor-benefit plan could keep their coverage to age 65 by having their share of cost deducted from their monthly annuity payments.

The option was offered from top management on down. All who were eligible received a letter of explanation from the president of the firm. The terminations were handled as routine retirements. Firm C7 analyzed the acceptance pattern and found that with a few exceptions, people were encouraged to retire about two years earlier than they had planned to retire. Our informant feels that this option caused the company "to lose a lot of good people, as well as those over the hill." There was some concern about losing talent when the option was first offered, but management was able to replace the early retirees without difficulty.

The firm is pleased with its program, and in the words of our informant, "it did not cost as much as it looks." He reports that if the firm had had to replace every early retiree, it would not have used this program. But only 60% of the 1,720 early retirees were replaced, and none of the refilled jobs was a salaried position. The program had another advantage in that it enabled the firm to continue hiring college graduates during three years when its competitors were unable to do so.

Most employees were content with the offer, although the firm received some complaints from persons who did not qualify. However, management did not let anyone back out of the decision once he had made it, and that caused a few problems. To avoid complaints, anyone who had retired early during the previous year was given the benefit of the plan if he met the eligibility criteria.

This company's experience shows that a successful program can be mounted quickly, if necessary. The program was designed within one month of the request from the president's office, formally placed on paper during the following two weeks, and announced the next month. Employees were given three months during which to elect the option.

Firm C8

This firm's formal early-retirement program was instituted in response to union pressure, not as a way to remove employees. The option is intended to permit employees with thirty years of service to retire even though they may not be 62 years of age. The program provides these employees a pension supplement from the time of early retirement until age 62. At that age, when the retiree can draw a reduced social-security benefit, the supplement is reduced about 50%.

In addition to this formal program, the firm has encouraged some people to leave with special pension arrangements. Others have been given the position of quasi-consultants. And still others, who were not eligible for an unreduced pension, have been given one anyway. These options are reportedly used very sparingly. Usually poor performers are counseled, placed in new positions, or encouraged to move to another firm while they are young.

Firms C9–C12

Besides the incentive of liberalized or suspended actuarial discounts for early retiree pensions, these firms provide a supplementary benefit tied to social security. The link to social security serves three purposes: (1) it makes possible an exact prediction of cost; (2) it establishes a definite cut-off point (usually age 62, occasionally 65); and (3) it enables the employee to view his early retirement as consistent with the retirement norms of society.

Firms C13–C18

These firms illustrate the type of incentive early-retirement schemes available at many firms. Employees whose age and years of service total a particular number may retire early without having their pensions actuarially reduced. Persons who retire before achieving this number have their pensions reduced, but they do not suffer the full reduction. These options make it possible for some employees to retire early, but they do not seem to attract many persons. The additional pension benefit is apparently not large enough to cause people to stop working, at least not until age 62. Sometimes pressure makes "early retirement" a euphemism for "severance."

At least a half-dozen issues must be considered when an incentive early-retirement scheme is designed: a minimum age for retirement eligibility, a minimum number of years of service, the consent of the organization, the period the option is in force, ease of funding, and the means of financing the supplement.

Industry has had extensive experience with incentive early-retirement schemes. A few larger firms have instituted formal programs. Many more corporations have special arrangements that are informal and not widely publicized. Some programs are offered for limited periods. Most effective in inducing early retirements are obviously those plans that pay the largest bonuses to persons who quit. They also appear to be the schemes most carefully administered and designed to respond to particular organizational goals. In the eyes of our informants, the most efficient arrangement has been the lump-sum severance payment offered for a fixed period.

A Minimum Age for Retirement Eligibility. A low minimum age results in an inadequate benefit level in most cases, but it may also provide a lifetime severance allowance for a relatively young employee. A low retirement age can also be a burden on the retirement system. Age 55 appears to be the youngest age at which most retirement plans in both industry and academia permit the payment of retirement benefits. For reasons of cost and level of benefits, few firms encourage incentive early-retirement prior to age 60.

A Minimum Number of Years of Service. Few conventional early-retirement plans permit retirement after fulfilling only a service-credit requirement, but both the minimum age for retirement and the number of years of service credit continue to decrease. Although some retirement plans permit retirement benefits to be paid after only five years, the benefits are quite limited, even when the employee has passed age 55. An increased-benefits early-retirement scheme, if it is to encourage more than a few retirements, would probably have to be limited to persons with at least ten years of service credit. Otherwise, the supplemental benefits would have to be substantial to compensate for the limited years of service credit and related employee and employer contributions.

Consent of the Organization. When eligibility requirements are liberal, the organization's consent is usually required. In some cases, the organization decides that an employee who might be eligible for early-retirement benefits does not merit an increased pension. In other cases, an organization might lose employees whose performance was at or above par, or it might pay a lifetime severance benefit to an employee who reemploys with another (possibly competing) organization. Sometimes organizational consent is required at younger ages but not older ages. Despite the usefulness to management of organizational consent, "window" options have been used to make early retirement available to all persons in certain age-service cohorts, in order to avoid possible charges of discrimination.

Period in Force. Some firms view these options as temporary; others, as permanent. In practice, all are temporary since they may be revised. Realizing that any option is temporary, employees may delay taking the option the first time offered in hopes that the program may be available at a later time when they feel they will be in a better position to take it. Due to these postponed retirements, the net result of a program might be only a negligible reduction in the age of retirement.

Ease of Funding. Basing an annuity supplement on a projection of future salary (or on present salary and stock-growth trends) is somewhat risky. A multiple of current salary as a termination benefit is more certain.

Means of Financing the Supplement. The provisions of the Employee Retirement Income Security Act (ERISA) and sections 403(b) and 415 of the Internal Revenue Code demand special attention to the way in which supplements are paid to persons who terminate or retire. Under the IRS code, there are limitations on the amounts that can be added to a person's annuity. (These issues are discussed at length in chapter 6.)

The key points in designing a scheme seem to be the minimum age for eligibility and the minimum number of years of service credit. Institutional consent, over and above what is implied in the design of the early-retirement option, is less widespread. Early retirement must be financed in some manner, either from the organization's general funds or through the pension contributions of current workers. The options include an influx of additional funds, a reduction in the number of employees, increases in the actuary tables, and a selective distribution of available funds among particular groups of workers. It would be possible for an institution to determine which employees have reached an age and length of service allowing their comfortable retirement while also leaving funds to finance a net increase in employees. However, these employees may not necessarily be the ones that the institution would like to retire. Further, selective early retirement may not be viewed as equitable. Instead, blanket availability of early retirement for age-service cohorts may be in order.

EARLY RETIREMENT IN THE FEDERAL GOVERNMENT[20]

Pension programs in the federal government are alleged to have generous provisions. The civil-service pension program is said to be so generous as to encourage early retirement. In this regard, the military retirement program also comes immediately to mind because of the early age at which many officers retire and because of its well-known "up-or-out" provision. These characteristics have prompted some college and university administrators to question whether similar retirement programs might be adopted to encourage faculty members to terminate early. Although academia may learn important lessons from the experience of these systems, there is little to suggest that their provisions could or should be copied by colleges and universities.

Early Retirement in the Civil Service

The Civil Service Retirement and Disability Fund covers nearly all civilian government employees, including all appointive and elective officers and employees in or under the executive, judicial, and legislative branches of the United States Government and the municipal government of the District of Columbia. Postal Service employees are also covered by the civil-service retirement system.[21] In 1976 almost 1.5 million people were drawing civil-service retirement benefits.[22]

In 1920, when the Civil Service Retirement Act became law, the government employed an abundance of superannuated employees. Many were in their eighties and nineties. At that time the goal of the newly formed retirement system was "to remove the aged and the disabled from government's active work force, and to do this in a socially acceptable way."[23] Although this is still the fundamental objective of the retirement program, and although the system *does not* include an incentive early-retirement plan, civil-service employees have tended to retire earlier and earlier.[24] The average retirement age dropped from 61.2 in 1964 to 58.1 in 1974. During the past ten years, there has also been a marked increase in involuntary retirements with reduced annuities at young ages.[25]

An employee must fulfill certain conditions before he is eligible for what the civil-service retirement system terms "optional retirement." He must meet one of three minimum conditions of age and service: (1) age 62 with five years of service; (2) age 60 with twenty years of service; or (3) age 55 with thirty years of service.[26] Having qualified in any one of these categories, the employee may have his annuity determined in the regular manner, the amount depending primarily upon length of service and average pay during the three years his salary was highest.

An employee may also be retired involuntarily when an agency is making a major staff cut, when a particular position is dissolved, or when an office or agency is liquidated.[27] In these situations the annuity is reduced by one-sixth of 1% for each full month the employee is under age 55. Early optional retirement is also available for employees whose duties are in law enforcement, firefighting, and air traffic control. These people can retire without reduction under age 55 after they have met certain requirements. Retirement due to disability may take place at a younger age if an employee becomes totally disabled and is unable to satisfactorily perform the duties of his position. He must also have completed at least five years of civilian service.[28]

In 1964 a survey was conducted of civil-service annuitants who had retired under the "55-30" optional-retirement provision. (Our search of the literature did not uncover a more recent survey.) The respondents were overwhelmingly positive about their early retirements despite the fact that they had retired with a permanent reduction in benefits.[29]

Early Retirement in the Military

In the military, promotion and retirement are intricately bound together. Personnel are regularly considered for promotion from one grade to another. Promotion is automatic to second lieutenant (in the Army, Marine Corps, and Air Force) and to ensign (in the Navy). After that point, promotion becomes a competitive process administered by the Selection Board.[30] At the lower ranks, an officer is separated if he fails selection twice. He receives his separation compensation, which is based on his number of years of commissioned service, in a lump sum.

The procedure changes slightly when a member of the Army, Air Force, or Marine Corps is attempting promotion from major to lieutenant colonel and when a Navy officer is attempting promotion from lieutenant commander to commander. If the officer is passed over twice at this step, he must be retired by his twentieth or twenty-first year of commissioned service. If promoted, he is guaranteed a position in the service until he reaches retirement eligibility. The pension received is 2-1/2% of base pay times the number of years of commissioned service. Similar procedures apply to the higher ranks, with slight differences among the services.

Military retirees tend to be young. If an individual retires upon completion of a normal career (twenty years), he may be in his early forties. Two things cause these young retirement ages. First, men ordinarily begin their military careers very young; officers are usually in their early twenties. Second, a person may retire voluntarily after only twenty years, knowing that he will receive full benefits. However, many of these relatively young men are retired because they have been separated from the service before they have progressed very far through the ranks. True, the less qualified are terminated, and it is contended that the "up-or-out" system maintains a "young, vigorous force."[31] One pertinent fact, though, is that those who are retired are also relatively young and vigorous.

"Up or out" also indirectly causes many voluntary retirements. An officer may choose to retire if he realizes that he has been performing poorly and will not be promoted at the next step. Perhaps to save face, or because he determines that the extra year or so he gains toward retirement benefits by staying until he is involuntarily separated will not compensate for what he could earn in civilian life, he decides to leave before he is told he must. For example, a naval captain with four years at Annapolis and twenty-four years active duty as a commissioned officer decided to retire at age 46. He saw little chance of being advanced to rear admiral. As he described it, the Navy had about 1,100 engineering duty officers. Each year only one or two, maybe three, made admiral. In his opinion, if he was going to have to leave the service and go into the business world, the younger the better.[32]

Is the captain's move to be considered early retirement? Perhaps not. Most military men retire between ages 40 and 50; military pensions are paid on the average at age 42.[33] These ages are considered "early" only outside the military. Indeed, there is some question concerning the appropriateness of the word "retirement" for these separations. Perhaps the term "mid-career change" more properly applies. Recall, though, that the military offers nothing to assist these persons in their mid-career change beyond some advice about retirement benefits and suggestions about establishing a second career.

The military retirement scheme is unlike any other. Most civilians do not work in jobs that offer promotions as frequently as a military career, nor does their continuing to work depend so completely upon their ability to rise in rank. A military retiree almost always needs to plan for a second career. This is not true for people who retire from private industry.

The military and civil-service retirement systems do not seem to hold much promise as models for academia. For one thing, their costs are skyrocketing.[34] Rep. Les Aspin of Wisconsin has called federal pension promises "the secret national debt."[35] Some upper-echelon civil-service employees have found it more profitable to retire than to continue working because until recently cost-of-living adjustments have exceeded salary increases.[36] The Department of Defense, concerned about extremely early retirements, has drafted proposals to "deliberalize" the current military retirement system. The main idea is to encourage military personnel to remain in service for thirty years by boosting the pension benefit formula during the third decade of service. The civil service and military do not want to encourage more early retirements. To do so would only place an ever-greater burden on an already troubled pension system.

Even with these problems, some persons have suggested the "up-or-out" system for academia. But the system probably would not help academia solve its immediate manpower problem because of the time lag involved. In fact, an "up-or-out" process which included hefty severance payments could place an unbelievable financial burden upon a college or university. One thing we can learn from the military and civil service is that business and industry may be right to use lump-sum severance payments to encourage early retirement. In that way, at least, the total cost of the extra payment is known in advance.

EARLY RETIREMENT IN ACADEMIA

Although many universities and colleges have had early retirement plans for decades, they generally only allow early retirement with a reduced annuity. Recently, though, institutions have made provisions for increases in early-retirement annuities to permit or even encourage persons to retire before the mandatory age.

During the growth years of the 1950s and 1960s, few universities and colleges had reason to consider ways in which to cause employees to retire early; they were having a difficult time recruiting and retaining them. Some institutions that had mandatory retirement provisions also had arrangements to re-hire over-age employees on a year to year basis.[37] Most persons who wanted to stay on after mandatory retirement were permitted to do so. Besides, at many institutions, mandatory retirement was as high as age 70. Some universities and colleges still set age 70 as the mandatory retirement age, and a few permit extensions beyond mandatory retirement; but in recent years the trend has been toward lower mandatory retirement ages and fewer extensions.[38] The reduction in the retirement age in academia is consistent with the reduction in the economy as a whole.[39] However, retirement ages in academia are still generally higher than those in industry, and a retirement considered "early" in academia might be considered "late" elsewhere.

In the early 1970s, Teachers Insurance and Annuity Association of America-College Retirement Equities Fund (TIAA-CREF) began to receive increased inquiries about early retirement. In 1972, TIAA-CREF prepared a document outlining a variety of provisions intended to supplement benefits for early retirees. These provisions were designed to make early retirement more attractive and to give institutions more flexibility in adjusting to staffing needs.[40]

In late 1972, TIAA-CREF sent a questionnaire to the business offices of 2,533 universities and colleges seeking information about their early-retirement practices.[41] Among the 1,294 institutions responding, over fifty reported providing some type of severance payment—including lump sum payments, a year's salary, a percentage of accrued sick leave, or a contribution to the pension fund to bring the early-retirement annuity up to what would have been received at mandatory retirement.

A reduced work-load option was reported by forty-four institutions. They were using this alternative both as an incentive to enter early retirement gradually and as a way to supplement the incomes of persons retiring early at reduced benefit rates. Some institutions also provided all or partial fringe benefits, including continued contributions to the pension fund until the mandatory retirement age, as part of this option.

Twenty-nine colleges reported programs that provided supplemental monthly retirement incomes for early retirees. Benefits (beyond those the early retirees would receive anyway) were provided by payments from current operating funds, additional premiums paid to individual annuities, group annuity arrangements, and special retirement funds and reserves. Other incentives included continued payment into social security, payment of health- and life-insurance premiums, and payment of pension fund contributions until the mandatory retirement age.

About the same time that TIAA-CREF administered its early-retirement survey, the Office of Institutional Analysis at the University of Virginia conducted a similar survey of the forty-eight member institutions of the Association of American Universities.[42] The University of Virginia study uncovered plans for reducing the mandatory retirement age to 65 in about half of the institutions. Most of the remaining institutions either already had begun- or were intending to begin- incentive early-retirement plans.

A follow-up survey of the University of Virginia sample was conducted during 1975 by the Office of Institutional Studies at the University of Southern California.[43] This survey found that early-retirement plans in universities had not changed much since the original study. The planned lowering of the mandatory retirement age had taken place at three institutions. Although some of the sample institutions were still considering changes in their plans, few changes had been made. Four universities had begun early-retirement programs, but eight had dropped their plans or were using them sporadically. Unfortunately, the reporting institutions were able to provide little information about the effectiveness of their early-retirement programs. Either they had not kept adequate records, or their plans had been in operation only a short while.

Other schemes were reported, including the payment of severance pay in a lump sum or in installments. Phasing into retirement through part-time employment was also discussed. Under this option, contributions to the employee's annuity would be continued at his full-time salary level so that his retirement income would be unaffected by his switch to part-time work. Another proposal provided an early-retirement supplement to persons retiring at least five years early. The supplement was calculated in a manner that allowed the larger supplement to those persons retiring the earliest.

These surveys provide sufficient data about most current early-retirement plans in academia. In order to discover the essential ingredients of incentive early-retirement schemes, we investigated in more detail the several plans that had encouraged faculty members to retire before the mandatory age. These five university plans are outlined in the following pages. In chapter 3, the experiences of persons retiring under four of these schemes and the schemes of two corporations are analyzed.

Institution A1

Until recently, early retirement at this institution was accomplished informally. There were no precise regulations concerning the eligibility age for early retirement or the number of years of service required. The faculty member retiring early received approximately 75% of the annuity that he would have received at the normal retirement age of 65. The cost of the supplemental annuity averaged about one-third of the total salary and benefits he would have been paid had he remained on the faculty until age 65. Individualized calculations were required to determine the amount of the annuity, which was dependent on the amount of the projected annuity at early retirement.

A standardized formula was recently developed to simplify calculations. The administration has decided to offer the standardized early-retirement annuity to staff members with at least ten years as members of the retirement plan and who will be at least 60 years of age and will have at least twenty years of service by July 1, 1977. The offer is being made only for early retirements to be effective either July 1, 1977; January 1, 1978; or July 1, 1978. The supplemental annuities will be purchased outside the regular retirement plan on a single-life basis without a spouse's benfit. The informal program will be continued for individuals age 55 to 60. Under both the formal and the informal program, the only restriction on employment is that the early retiree may not be reemployed at the university.

This university formalized its incentive early-retirement plan to create an option for long-service employees who would otherwise be laid off, to give long-service pensions to senior faculty and staff who wanted to retire for personal reasons, and to encourage marginal performers to retire.

Institution A2

At Institution A2, where the mandatory retirement age is 70, a faculty member may retire at any age between 65 and 70. His early-retirement benefit is equal to what he would have received had he waited until age 70 to retire, but *without* a salary change. During the early retirement years, he receives benefit payments directly from the university, which makes full contributions to his annuity. When he reaches age 70, the university contributions cease. He then begins to draw his annuity. Eligibility is limited to employees with at least twenty years of service and eighteen years of retirement-plan participation.

Under the terms of the early-retirement plan, any retiree who "resumes gainful employment" anywhere while he is still receiving interim benefits directly from the university (i.e., prior to age 70) will forfeit those benefits as long as he is employed. There seems to be no standard interpretation, however, of what constitutes "gainful employment."

This university launched its early-retirement plan two decades ago when it realized some people reaching the mandatory retirement age had pensions too low to provide for an adequate retirement. Although age 65 had been intended as the "normal" retirement age, most people could not afford to retire before the compulsory age of 70. Concerned that it was penalizing long-service employees, the university devised what might be called a career-service supplement. The plan does have an element of inducement, but most people see it as a bonus for twenty years of service.

Institution A3

The scheme at this university involves early retirement *plus* part-time employment. When a professor decides to retire early, he receives the actuarial equivalent of the benefits due him under the normal early-retirement program. In addition, during the period between early retirement and mandatory retirement, he is given part-time employment which brings his total income up to the annuity he would have received had he remained employed at his current salary until the mandatory retirement age. At the mandatory retirement age the part-time employment ceases, and the early-retirement benefits are supplemented by an annuity purchased by the university. Thus, at the mandatory retirement age, the early retiree continues to receive an income equal to the annuity he would have received had he remained fully employed until mandatory retirement.

Institution A4

The plan at this institution was a response to a high proportion of tenured faculty members who severely restricted the school's ability to hire new academics. An early-retirement plan was seen as a way to increase turnover in the faculty.

The plan was based upon the premise that early retirement should be open to all older faculty members at their own initiative, not offered on an ad hoc basis to certain persons. The plan's designers reasoned that the best candidates for early retirement were those persons with lower-than-average salaries for their age and length-of-service groups. Assuming that one's salary is an indication of relative productivity, the plan calculates the early-retirement benefit on the basis of the median earnings for one's age and service category. It therefore offers a great financial incentive to retire to the lower-salaried employees. Although the plan has been in operation for several years, it has encouraged only a half dozen persons to retire.

Institution A5

The mandatory retirement age at Institution A5 is 70. In 1971, however, an "accelerated retirement program" was implemented, not so much as a way to encourage people to retire early as a means of supplementing the inadequate pensions some retirees were receiving. The program originated in the faculty senate, where its supporters argued that all faculty members should be financially able to retire at age 65. The resulting senate resolution also noted that faculty members should be encouraged to voluntarily fix a date for retirement far enough in advance to permit effective personal retirement planning and the orderly replacement of retiring professors. If a faculty member fixes his retirement at age 65, the university will match an increased payment into his retirement account. If he then fails to retire at age 65, the university stops its contributions to his pension account.

Recent changes in the provisions of the option permit an employee to accelerate contributions to his annuity program during any ten-year period between ages 52 and 65, but not beyond age 65. There is some confusion about the purpose of the option. Clearly, a primary factor was concern for faculty members faced with the choice of retiring on inadequate pensions or remaining on the faculty until an advanced age because of financial need. But the scheme is also seen by some as a way to encourage less productive faculty members to retire early.

This program is unusual in that it requires the participating faculty member to fix his retirement date ten years in advance. He may elect to stay on past that date without the university's consent, but the university can cease its contributions to his annuity program. Once a person does retire and begins drawing his annuity, there is no restriction on employment at the university or elsewhere.

More than four-hundred faculty members have opted for the accelerated retirement program, but as of July 1, 1977, only ninety had reached their specified retirement dates. In the last several years, it is estimated, about one-third of those who reached their retirement dates continued on in their university positions, although sometimes they worked part-time or only for an extra year. That no attempt has been made to see whether participants do indeed retire on schedule reflects how little this program is considered a means of encouraging early retirement.

We investigated the increased-benefit early-retirement arrangements of several other universities, but none of those options had been implemented or had retired more than a few persons. One institution developed an arrangement whereby it would make a payment to the early retiree's annuity program so that his early annuity would equal what he would have received by staying on until the mandatory retirement age. The arrangement was never formalized. It was offered to only a few individuals and has not been promoted or discussed on campus. Another institution devised a scheme involving early retirement and reemployment, but the state retirement system is blocking implementation of the option. Grossly underfunded, the system could run into the red if many persons took even normal early retirement.

CONCLUSION

We have focused on only two career options—mid-career retraining and early retirement—but there are few other options for overstaffed universities and for faculty members in glutted fields or with outdated skills. From the university's perspective, the options, short of firing a professor, include finding some new way to use his skills (shift him into administration), giving him new skills to use elsewhere (mid-career retraining), or paying him to retire early (incentive early retirement). The professor's options are similar and include identifying new tasks or challenges that can be met with current skills, learning new skills that make him employable in a setting where jobs are available, or retiring if he can afford it.

Individuals have changed careers through each of these means, but most shifts to date have occurred informally and at the individual's initiative. Industry and academia have implemented formal career change programs, but both sectors have had far more experience with incentive early retirement: those actions taken to encourage people to retire earlier than usual. These schemes promise to open university ranks to new faculty members with needed skills, to free money for new hiring, and to improve morale. Later chapters will deal with the fiscal and staffing questions, but first the human consequences of induced early retirement will be investigated.

NOTES

1. Herbert E. Coolidge and Alton L. Taylor, "Consideration for Faculty Retirement Policies in a Steady-State Condition: A Report to the Provost," mimeo. (Charlottesville, Virginia: University of Virginia, Office of Institutional Analysis, June 1973); Hans H. Jenny, *Early Retirement, A New Issue in Higher Education: The Financial Consequences of Early Retirement* (New York: TIAA—CREF, 1974); Stanford University, *The Faculty Early Retirement Program* (Stanford, California: 1973); Subcommittee on Early Retirement, "An Early Retirement Plan for the University of

Colorado," mimeo. (Boulder, Colorado: University of Colorado, 1974); Teachers Insurance and Annuity Association of America—College Retirement Equities Fund, "Survey of Early Retirement Practices of Colleges and Universities," mimeo. (New York: TIAA—CREF, 1973); and Veronica Tincher, "Early Retirement Plans in Higher Education," mimeo. (Los Angeles: University of Southern California, Office of Institutional Studies, January 1976).

2. Joseph Zelan conducted the research on which this section of the chapter is based.

3. Ana L. Zambrano and Alan D. Entine, *A Guide to Career Alternatives for Academics* (New Rochelle, N.Y.: Change Magazine Press, 1976).

4. Anthony H. Pascal et al., *An Evaluation of Policy-Related Research on Programs for Mid-Life Career Redirection,* 2 vols. (Santa Monica, California: Rand Corp., 1975).

5. Pascal et al., *Evaluation,* vol. 2, pp. 140–144.

6. Pascal et al., *Evaluation.*

7. Velma M. Thompson, "Unemployed Aerospace Professionals: Lessons for Programs for Mid-Life Career Redirection," *Policy Analysis* 3, no. 3 (Summer 1977): 375–385.

8. This information on military retirement and preretirement counseling was provided by Colonel Kirby Vick, Retired Officers Association, Washington, D.C.

9. M. J. Fox, Jr., and E. G. Lambert, "Air Traffic Controllers: Struggle for Recognition and Second Careers," *Public Personnel Management* 3, no. 3 (May/June 1974): 75–80.

10. Personal communication from Mr. Michael Simons of the Professional Air Traffic Controllers Association.

11. For listings of such programs see: *A Selected List of Major Fellowship Opportunities and Aids to Advanced Education for United States Citizens* (Washington, D.C.: National Research Council, 1976); and *A Directory of Public Service Internships: Opportunities for the Graduate, Post Graduate and Mid Career Professional* (Washington, D.C.: National Center for Public Service Internship Programs, 1976).

12. Charles B. Neff, "Faculty Retraining: A Four State Perspective," paper presented at the 1978 National Conference on Higher Education (Chicago: March 1978).

13. Although we have data on the cases of specific individuals, the details are not important enough to risk revealing the identity of persons involved in the retraining programs.

14. Velma M. Thompson, "A Government Policy to Induce Efficient Retraining During Unemployment." (Santa Monica: The Rand Corp., 1977).

15. "NSF Sets Its Sights," *Change* 9, no. 8 (August 1977): 47.

16. Mitchell Meyer and Harland Fox, *Early Retirement Programs* (New York: The Conference Board, 1971), pp. 1-2.

17. Mitchell Meyer and Harland Fox, *Profile of Employee Benefits* (New York: The Conference Board, 1974), pp. 52-55. See also Towers, Perrin, Forster and Crosby, *Early Retirement for Executives: Practices, Attitudes and Trends* (New York: Towers, Perrin, Forster and Crosby, 1974).

18. Meyer and Fox, *Early Retirement Programs,* pp. 19-36.

19. Towers, Perrin, Forster and Crosby, *Early Retirement for Executives.*

20. Gretchen West Patton conducted the research on which this section of the chapter is based.

21. U.S. Congress, House of Representatives, *Public Law 91-375, the Postal Reorganization Act, H.R. 17070,* 91st. Cong., 12 August, 1970, p. 14.

22. "Pensions for Federal Workers: $17 Billion and Soaring," *U.S. News and World Report* 79, no. 15 (13 October, 1975): 85.

23. Andrew E. Ruddock, "Salute to Progress: Civil Service Retirement System 1920-1970," *Civil Service Journal* 10, no. 4 (June 1970): 20.

24. U.S. Civil Service Commission, Bureau of Retirement, Insurance, and Occupational Health, *Survey of Voluntary Retirement Age Provisions of Selected Public and Private Employers* (Washington, D.C.: May 1975) p. 1.

25. Leonore E. Bixby, "Retirement Patterns in the United States: Research and Policy Interaction," *Social Security Bulletin,* August 1976, p. 9.

26. *Your Retirement System, Pamphlet 18: Questions and Answers Concerning the Federal Civil Service Retirement Law* (Washington, D.C.: U.S. Government Printing Office, July 1975), p. 14.

27. Bixby, "Retirement Patterns," p. 9.

28. *Your Retirement System,* p. 15.

29. Bixby, "Retirement Patterns," pp. 9-10; and Elizabeth F. Messer, "Thirty-Eight Years Is A Plenty," *Civil Service Journal* 5, no. 2 (October/December 1964): 24.

30. *United States Code* II, 1970 edition (Washington, D.C.: U.S. Government Printing Office, 1971): 1302, 1581-1605, 1809-1841, and 1991-2010. Supplementary information about military promotion and retirement was provided by Colonel Richard Alger, Officer Personnel Management Section, Office of the Deputy Assistant Secretary for Military Personnel Policy, Department of Defense.

31. Colonel Minter L. Wilson, Jr., "Representative Aspin Continues Attacks on Military," *The Retired Officer* 33, no. 1 (January 1977): 4.

32. Israel Shenker, "A Navy Captain Finds a Job Ashore," *The Retired Officer* 33, no. 1 (January 1977): 18.

33. Les Aspin, *Guns or Pensions: A Study of the Military Retired Pay System* (Washington, D.C.: U.S. House of Representatives, November 1976), p. 5.

34. "Promises, Promises, Promises," *Forbes,* 15 August 1975, pp. 52–53.

35. Aspin, *Guns or Pensions,* p. 2.

36. Aspin, *Guns or Pensions,* p. 34; "The Hidden Costs of Federal Pensions," *Business Week,* 27 April 1974, p. 28; and "When It Costs Money to Keep on Working," *U.S. News and World Report,* 24 November 1975, p. 27.

37. Some institutions have had flexible-age retirement plans which permit extensions beyond the stated normal or base retirement age. Now that college faculties have stopped growing, many flexible-age plans no longer permit extensions beyond the base year. For an overview of flexible-age plans, see Francis P. King, "Retirement-Age Experience Under Flexible-Age Retirement Plans, 1930–1970," *AAUP Bulletin* 56, no. 1 (March 1970); 14–19. If mandatory retirement is abolished, persons may need to plan for flexible retirement. See James W. Walker, "Are You Ready for Flexible Retirement?" mimeo. (New York: Towers, Perrin, Forster and Crosby, 1977).

38. Coolidge and Taylor, "Faculty Retirement Policies"; and Tincher, "Early Retirement Plans."

39. *Manpower Report of the President* (Washington, D.C.: U.S. Government Printing Office, 1975), p. 205.

40. Teachers Insurance and Annuity Association of America—College Retirement Equities Fund, *Provisions for Early Retirement* (New York: TIAA—CREF, 1972). This bulletin was also published as William T. Slater, "Early Retirement: Some Questions and Some Options," *Journal of Higher Education* 58, no. 3 (October 1972): 559–566.

41. TIAA—CREF, "Survey of Early Retirement Practices of Colleges and Universities," mimeo. (New York: TIAA—CREF, 1973).

42. Coolidge and Taylor, "Faculty Retirement Policies."

43. Tincher, "Early Retirement Plans."

3

Experiences of Incentive Early Retirees[1]

Academics apparently accept retirement as part of their life cycle,[2] and most are satisfied with their lives during retirement.[3] Many even look forward to retiring.[4] Retired professors tend to be in good health and have relatively good incomes,[5] two key variables affecting retirement satisfaction.[6] Their generally positive feelings derive in part from the relative ease with which they are able to continue their academic lives during retirement. Most retired academics do not shut themselves off entirely from their former lives.[7] Emeritus professors are involved in a variety of activities, many continuing those academic pursuits they enjoyed most while employed, others pursuing new non-academic interests.[8]

During the past decade, researchers have found retired professors willing to return to research related to their preretirement research.[9] Others have discovered that retired academics want gainful part-time employment.[10] Yet most former professors want to return to work not because of financial need but because they would enjoy doing so.[11] Several recent studies indicate the extent of academic reemployment. Alan Rowe found that 40% of retired academics are employed, most of them in teaching or research.[12] In a nationwide study of its annuitants, Teachers Insurance and Annuity Association-College Retirement Equities Fund (TIAA-CREF) found that 48% of its respondents had worked for pay after retirement. Retired faculty members and administrators were more likely to report employment after retirement than were non-academic annuitants.[13] In a study of recent University of California

57

retirees, 44% reported reemployment, and 84% of these persons were satisfied with the amount they were working.[14]

These data show the widespread desire of researchers and teachers to maintain their academic lives and even to continue in some line of related employment. What do these attitudes mean for retirement schemes aimed at getting academics to retire early? How likely is it that these persons will agree to retire early? What has happened to those who have retired early? Are they any less satisfied than other retirees? Since widespread early retirement in academia is a recent phenomenon, little nationwide information is available to answer these questions. We do have, however, data from a study of recent retirees of the University of California in which the experiences of professors who voluntarily retired early are compared with the experiences of those who retired at the mandatory age.[15]

Since 1968, more than 40% of the full-time faculty members who retired from the University of California did so before reaching the mandatory age, and the early retirees tend to be more satisfied with their retirement decisions than the mandatory-age retirees. Furthermore, the early retirees reported overwhelmingly that, if they had it to do all over again, they would still retire early. Current employees plan to retire at about the same average age as recent retirees, and those planning to retire early are much more likely to look forward to retirement than persons planning to retire at the mandatory age.

Perhaps the most important finding of this and several other recent studies is that even if mandatory retirement were abolished, many faculty members would consider retiring early under the right conditions. The University of California study found that 21% of the mandatory-age retirees and 33% of the early retirees would have retired earlier if they had been offered a more attractive early-retirement plan. At all ages of retirement, the primary condition was a larger annuity. As an inducement, part-time employment ran a poor second. Sixty-eight percent of current employees reported that they also would retire earlier than they now planned to if offered a larger pension and—less important—part-time employment.

Since the University of California study was conducted, other researchers have obtained similar results. A study of University of Southern California faculty members found that 28% of recent retirees would have preferred to retire earlier under a more advantageous plan, and 75% of current faculty members would consider early retirement with appropriate financial incentives.[16]

A nationwide survey of academics discovered similar feelings.[17] Two-thirds of the survey's respondents would consider retiring earlier than they now plan if they were assured of pension benefits equal to those they would receive at mandatory retirement. Here too, part-time employment was the second most important condition for early retirement.

Many of the faculty members who now speak favorably of early retirement might not take advantage of a plan if it were offered to them. Nonetheless, these data suggest that a sizable portion of today's academics who are not now planning to retire early might agree to do so *under the right conditions*. Offered an increased annuity and part-time employment arrangements, some faculty members have agreed to retire early.

We conducted extensive personal interviews with individuals who had retired under special incentive early-retirement provisions. Through these interviews we hoped to obtain a consumer report, so to speak, about induced or incentive early retirement. We hoped to find out when and how the respondents decided to retire early, why they did so, and how satisfied they were with their decision. We also wanted to know whether early retirement had affected their financial well-being, their professional activity, and their general activity and happiness. Finally, we sought to know how they had prepared themselves for early retirement, what advice they would give to others considering early retirement, and how they would evaluate the early-retirement programs at their own institutions.

THE INCENTIVE EARLY RETIREES[18]

Potential respondents for the study were identified by the administrators of the special incentive early-retirement programs at four universities and two corporations. (For reasons of confidentiality, these institutions cannot be identified. We will refer to the academic institutions as A1 through A4 and to the corporations as C1 and C2.) Although we requested the names of all faculty or managerial and professional staff who had retired under the special options, institutions A1, A4, C1, and C2 preferred to make the first contact with potential respondents themselves, relaying to us the names of only those who consented to answer our questions. We intended to interview all the retirees whose names we were given. However, we took a random sample of 60% of the retirees from institution A2 because it had many more potential respondents than the other institutions.

Altogether, we interviewed seventy incentive early retirees, of whom fifty-two were from the four universities (Table 2). Sixty of the interviews were conducted especially for this study between October, 1976, and February, 1977. Ten were conducted in 1975 as part of an earlier study.[19] The interviews averaged just under two hours and were conducted in the retiree's home or office. Twelve interviews were conducted by telephone, with no noticeable differences in length or depth of response. The interviews were structured informally, according to an interview guide reproduced in the appendix. Nearly all the responses were open-ended and were coded after the interview.

Forty percent of the retired faculty members were from the sciences (including the social sciences); 43% were from the professions; and only 15% were from the humanities. One respondent was a nonteaching librarian. The scientists included seven from engineering; two each from chemistry and the biological sciences; and one each from physics, zoology, and plant physiology. Among former social scientists were

Table 2 Interviewee Participation by Institution

| Institutions | Number of Special-Incentive Early Retirees | | | |
	Retired from the Institution	Contacted for Participation	Interviewed	Percentage of Potential Respondents Interviewed
Academic				
A1	16	16	6	38
A2	56	33	29	52
A3	16	16	15	94
A4	6	6	2	33
Subtotal	94	71	52	55
Corporate				
C1	*	11	9	*
C2	*	9	9	*
Subtotal	*	20	18	*
Total	*	91	70	*

*Data not available

three economists, two anthropologists, one political scientist, and one psychologist. The professionals' fields included education, physical education, business, medicine, nursing, dentistry, public health, journalism, library science, and social work. Respondents from the humanities represented English, French, German, history, classics, and fine arts. We made no attempt to select respondents by field because of the relatively small pool of respondents. Furthermore, we did not weight the responses to adjust for sampling and response rates or to produce population estimates. The sampling procedure prohibited such adjustments. Most of the interviewees had retired very recently. In fact, 69% of the academic retirees and 89% of the retirees from business had retired no more than two years before they were interviewed. Nevertheless, six retirees in the study had retired from five to ten years before the interview, and we found no systematic differences between their responses and those who had retired more recently.

By current American standards, the subjects had not retired very early; nearly half (49%) were age 65 or older at retirement (Table 3). There was a marked difference between the average retirement ages of the corporate and academic retirees, however: 59.6 for the retirees from business and 64.0 for the academic retirees. Eighty percent of the aca-

Table 3 Age at Retirement

| Institutions | Age | | | | | |
	55–59	60–62	63–64	65–66	67–70	Total[a]
Academic			Percentages			
A1	50	50	0	0	0	100 (6)
A2	0	3	0	83	14	100 (29)
A3	13	13	33	40	0	100 (15)
A4	0	0	100	0	0	100 (2)
Subtotal	10	12	14	58	8	100 (52)
Corporate						
C1	22	44	33	0	0	100 (9)
C2	56	44	0	0	0	100 (9)
Subtotal	39	44	17	0	0	100 (18)
Total	17	20	14	43	6	100 (70)

Note: Row percentages do not always sum to 100% because of rounding.

[a]Number of respondents upon which row percentages are based is shown in parentheses.

demics, but only 17% of the corporate retirees, were over age 62 at the time of retirement.

An institution's mandatory-retirement regulations obviously influence the age of retirement. On the average, both the academic and the corporate retirees terminated four to five years before their respective mandatory ages. However, because of the higher mandatory-retirement age for most of the academic retirees (age 70 at institution A2 and age 67 at institution A3), the retired academics tended to be older at the time of retirement.

In spite of having retired younger, the corporate retirees tended to have been employed longer by the firms from which they had retired; 72% of these retirees had thirty or more years of service, compared with only 34% of the academic retirees. This difference is partly the result of the relatively older ages at which academics are first retained by institutions and also of their tendency to move among institutions during their careers.

The early-retirement eligibility requirements set by an institution also help determine the age of retirement. In our survey, the effects of such requirements are most evident where retirement decisions were generally voluntary—i.e., at institutions A2, C1, and C2. Most of the early retirees from these institutions retired almost immediately after meeting the age and service requirements for special early retirement. At institution A2, where the early retirement eligibility requirements were 65 years of age and twenty years of service (plus eighteen years of participation in the retirement plan), only 31% of the early retirees continued working after establishing eligibility on both criteria. At institution C1, where eligibility was established after age 58 with thirty years of service, only 22% of the early retirees passed this point. The special incentive arrangement at institution C2 was a limited time "open window" which had been offered twice in the past five years to anyone with twenty-five years of service. The early retiree received half-pay for four years on top of his regular early retirement pension *if* he was 55 or older. If he was under 55, he got only the special severance payment. Only 33% of the early retirees had passed up the "open window" the first time they were eligible for both the special payment and a pension.

THE DECISION TO RETIRE EARLY

Few of the interviewees had made long-range plans to retire early. In fact, over half of them (58%) had begun thinking seriously about early retirement less than four years before their decision, and 29% had been seriously considering it for less than two years. Only 21% of the respondents had been planning to retire early for more than ten years. At institution A1, whose special incentive program was the least voluntary and newest among all six institutions, our respondents made their retirement decision in the shortest time: less than two years for all six. Nearly one-third of the retired faculty members from institution A2, where mandatory retirement was age 70 and the twenty-year old early-retirement plan for those aged 65 was strictly voluntary, nearly one third said they had "always" expected to retire early.[20] The respondents were quite candid in their descriptions of why they decided to retire early.

> *I was not on the forefront of work, and I had worked since [my childhood]. I was looking at others who were old; and I was not convinced they were very effective. I felt one of the best contributions a person could make would be to get out of the way of others. (University A3, respondent #16, social science field)*

> *When early retirement came out, there were two factors. [This campus] was faced with decreasing its faculty by [a specific number]. In my department there were two brilliant young faculty members, and I was sure the department would take a one FTE cut. I had in mind that I would hate to see one of these men cut, but if early retirement had not worked out, I would not have retired. There were also problems in the department . . . internal strife. . . . I welcomed the opportunity to get out. . . . I wanted to release [relieve] the day-to-day tension. (A3–12, humanities)*

> *I found that I did not enjoy teaching much, and I started to experience [a particular physical problem], so the early-retirement plan was attractive. I retired two years early. I was so near to the normal age that there was really no difference. I saw early retirement as a way to get out of two years of pain. (A4–2, profession)*

> *I considered it even before there was special compensation . . . I had a couple of large academic projects that I wanted to finish, and I already had a house in [another state]. I wanted to get away . . . I had worked twenty-seven years at [this university], continuously from 1946 to 1973. . . . It was not out of a sense of disenchantment with the university or profession. It was a personal consideration regarding my writing. (A4–1, humanities)*

The reasons for retiring early were quite varied, and although there were minor differences among institutions, there was almost no difference between retired academics and retired corporate employees (Table 4). That is, the rank order of reasons for retiring early, determined by how frequently they were mentioned, was nearly identical for retirees from academic institutions and retirees from business.

Most of the early retirees mentioned several factors which influenced their decision.[21] The most common reason (mentioned by 49%) was that they had already developed, or else wanted to develop, some interests outside their regular work-related responsibilities. Often the academics had a specific project in mind, such as finishing a book or a research project. Others said they retired to set new goals for themselves and to enjoy an altogether different life-style. The next most frequently stated reason (mentioned by 43%) was that they had lost interest in or no longer enjoyed their work, or else they were fatigued by the pressures that accompanied even the most enjoyable challenges. Some of the early retirees (31%) said they saw little reason to continue, since they already had enough money to retire comfortably. In 30% of the cases, the special incentive arrangement had encouraged the interviewee to retire early. (There was no double-counting these last two reasons. That is, we separated being offered an attractive arrangement that made early retirement financially feasible from having enough money to retire regardless of one's retirement plan. If one considers these situations essentially the same, then being financially able to retire becomes the primary reason for early retirement.) One-fifth of the early retirees said a health problem or disability had contributed to their early retirement, and 17% said they felt they had worked long enough and deserved a change or rest. Other reasons were mentioned less frequently.

Asked, "Whom did you talk to about when to retire?" both academic and corporate retirees mentioned spouses most often and then their superiors.[22] Twelve percent of the respondents said they had discussed their decision with no one. The retirees who discussed their decision with the administrators of their retirement system were noticeably few (only 14%). This only means, however, that they did not seek advice from the retirement system on *when* to retire. Many did in fact go to the retirement office for information on financial matters and other details of the arrangement before making their decision.

SATISFACTION WITH THE DECISION

Ninety-eight percent of the early retirees said they were either satisfied or very satisfied with their decision to retire early. Only one retiree

Table 4 Reasons for Retiring Early

Age at Retirement	To devote time to or develop other interests; to change general lifestyle	Decreased interest in or satisfaction from work; too much pressure working	Able to financially; finances good enough, as good, or even better	Availability or attractiveness of special early-retirement options	Health problems, disabilities, or perceived dangers to health	Worked long enough; ready for a rest or a change	Dissatisfaction or disagreement with management or focus of department/organization	Dissatisfaction with quality of own performance	Encouragement from spouse	Pressure from a supervisor	To free a position; to turn over responsibilities to a younger person	To leave at one's "peak"; to retire on one's own initiative	Had to retire anyway from administrative post	Commute too inconvenient	To move to another climate	To obtain a more flexible work schedule	Total
							Percentages										
Academics																	
67–70	75	50	75	0	25	25	0	0	0	0	0	0	0	0	0	0	[a] (4)
65–66	50	37	20	30	17	23	10	20	10	7	7	13	13	3	3	7	[a] (30)
63–64	57	43	29	29	43	14	14	14	14	0	0	0	0	0	17	0	[a] (7)
60–62	50	33	33	0	17	0	0	0	17	33	20	0	0	0	0	0	[a] (6)
55–59	20	60	40	60	20	0	40	20	0	20	0	0	0	0	0	0	[a] (5)
Subtotal	50	40	29	27	21	17	12	15	10	10	6	8	8	2	4	4	[a] (52)
Corporate Employees[b]																	
63–64	33	67	100	0	33	33	0	0	0	0	0	0	0	0	0	0	[a] (3)
60–62	75	13	25	38	13	13	25	0	25	13	14	0	0	0	13	0	[a] (8)
55–59	14	86	29	57	14	14	0	0	0	6	6	0	0	29	0	0	[a] (7)
Subtotal	44	50	39	39	17	17	11	0	11	6	6	0	0	11	6	0	[a] (18)
Total	49	43	31	30	20	17	11	11	10	9	6	6	6	4	4	3	[a] (70)

[a]Because respondents were able to cite more than one reason, the rows add up to more than 100%.

[b]No corporate employees retired at or above age 65.

Table 5   Satisfaction with the Decision to Retire Early

Age at Retirement	Very Dissatisfied	Dissatisfied	Satisfied	Very Satisfied	Total
Academics			Percentages		
67–70	0	0	25	75	100 (4)
65–66	0	0	30	70	100 (30)
63–64	0	0	0	100	100 (4)
60–62	0	17	0	83	100 (6)
55–59	0	0	40	60	100 (5)
Subtotal	0	2	25	73	100 (49)
Corporate Employees					
63–64	0	0	33	67	100 (3)
60–62	0	0	38	63	100 (8)
55–59	0	0	14	86	100 (7)
Subtotal	0	0	28	72	100 (18)
Total	0	2	25	73	100 (67)

Note: Missing observations (MO) = 3.

said he was dissatisfied (Table 5). Seventy-three percent said they were very satisfied. The overwhelming positiveness of this response might lead some to wonder whether the respondents were being candid with us or whether they had rationalized their decisions. Given their openness on many topics, as well as their enthusiastic comments, this possibility seems unlikely.

> *It has enabled me to complete my book, which took me longer than I thought. Monetarily, the income has been O.K. I haven't missed the few dollars' difference between my income and my salary. . . . Oh, it's enabled me to do some other things besides the book: travel, which I've always enjoyed. I've certainly been pleased to be relieved of the pressures and difficulties of teaching. . . . Students are quite different from the ones in our earlier classes. . . . People sometimes say, "Don't you miss the students?" Well, in a way, but not to the extent where I wish I was back teaching them. (A2–35, profession)*

> *I think it was an ideal situation, and I would go so far as to recommend that other faculty and staff consider it seriously. [Early retirement with part-time employment] permits the faculty member to gradually taper off his responsibilities and still maintain a financial status which is acceptable. So many times people work full-time up to a certain Friday night and after that it's nothing. It's a step func-*

tion, and in many cases it's a disaster. It's too abrupt a change. (A3-4, science)

I now very seldom go to campus. I don't know a single student. . . . I returned to see changes in students. It was hard to adjust to pickets outside of the classroom. To see such disruption was a shock. . . . I always wanted time to read. Now I go to the library twice a week and read a book a day. . . . I find it a struggle to go down to the office once a month. . . . I [answer correspondence] in half a day. I got out of a job I didn't like. (A4-2, profession)

We have made a considerable change of life, and we are enjoying it to the hilt. . . . We're enjoying the outdoors immensely, becoming beach bums almost. . . . Also, we haven't made a complete change from our former lives. I'm working on a book, and my wife has writing projects; so it hasn't been a complete change of life. It's just that now, when we write, it's because we want to. . . . We've had no reason to question the decision to retire early. As a matter of fact, the joy of it increases every day. (A2-24, humanities)

I can advertise retirement for anybody. I think it's great! (A1-1, science)

I've lost something, but I anticipated that. And I've gained something. The loss is your contact with students. . . . The gain, of course, is that your time is all your own. And also that I'm not trying to do something like lecturing that I'm not fit for. (A2-7, humanities)

I had a strong feeling for some time, looking at my friends and other people, that the sixties are still good years, that you don't start developing problems until later, and that if you have things you want to do, the best time to do them is in your sixties. And you can't do that when you're tied down to a position. . . . And I had some other interests. I had a strong feeling that one should retire young enough to develop some new interests, too. Not to be solely dependent on your job for intellectual stimulation. (A2-13, profession)

It's a tremendous release of tension . . . It's turning a new page, in a way. . . . Americans are too conditioned to strive for success, for a big paycheck. Life's too short to just wear yourself down and not be able to reap the other benefits of life besides drawing a huge salary. I think the key to the thing is whether you think you're making a contribution and living up to your own expectations. It's important not to fool yourself about this just in order to pull down a fat paycheck. (A3-6, profession)

I enjoy the freedom. . . . I know a lot of cases where people didn't live very long after they retired, where they worked up to age 65. If you enjoy your work so much, and if it's the only thing you have, that's not so bad. But, if you have other things you would like to do, but you're waiting until age 65 to get the full retirement benefits and then you never live to reap the advantages of those benefits, then you've had it. (Corporation C1, respondent #8, supervisor)

The point is, you don't have the pressure of thinking, "I've got to get up. I've got to get dressed. I've got to go to work and face that stack of papers that was there yesterday." I like the feeling of independence, that I can do what I want for a change and not what I'm forced to do. As a result, I've done various things that I couldn't do before. (C2-3, manager)

We also asked the interviewees, "If you could make the decision again—under the same circumstances but knowing what you now know—would you retire at the same time, earlier, or later?" Only five of the early retirees said they would retire later if they had it to do again, and four said they would retire sooner (Table 6). Among the academic retirees, 90% said they would retire at the same time.

Table 6   Retirement Decision if Made Again

Age at Retirement	Would Retire Earlier	Would Retire At the Same Time	Would Retire Later	Total
		Percentages		
Academics				
67–70	25	75	0	100 (4)
65–66	3	90	7	100 (30)
63–64	20	80	0	100 (5)
60–62	0	100	0	100 (6)
55–59	0	100	0	100 (7)
Subtotal	6	90	4	100 (50)
Corporate Employees				
63–64	0	100	0	100 (3)
60–62	13	63	25	100 (8)
55–59	0	86	14	100 (7)
Subtotal	6	78	17	100 (18)
Total	6	87	7	100 (68)

Note: MO = 2.

Finally, we queried: "Would you have retired earlier *under the right conditions*? That is, is there anything the university (or the company) could have done to encourage you to retire earlier than you did?" Seventy percent of the academics and 53% of the corporate early retirees said no, they would not have retired earlier, even if the conditions had been different. Those who gave reasons said they would not have been psychologically ready for retirement or they were too involved in their work. On the other hand, about one-third of the early retirees said they would have retired earlier if the conditions had made it *financially* feasible—if, for example, the special option had been available to them earlier or if the annuity had been larger.

THE EFFECTS OF EARLY RETIREMENT

Financial Well-Being

The early retirees seemed to be faring well financially. According to 84% of the respondents, there had been no change in their standard of living since retirement (Table 7). Although their gross income was lower,

Table 7 Current Standard of Living Compared with that Before Retirement

Age at Retirement	Lower than Before Retirement	Same	Higher than Before Retirement	Total
Academics		Percentages		
67–70	0	100	0	100 (4)
65–66	3	83	13	100 (30)
63–64	20	80	0	100 (5)
60–62	0	100	0	100 (6)
55–59	0	100	0	100 (5)
Subtotal	4	88	8	100 (50)
Corporate Employees				
63–64	0	100	0	100 (3)
60–62	0	75	25	100 (8)
55–59	0	57	43	100 (7)
Subtotal	0	72	28	100 (18)
Total	3	84	13	100 (68)

Note: MO = 2.

they said their "spendable" income was higher. There were no deductions for social security. They did not have to pay income tax on their social-security checks or on income from their own after-tax contributions to retirement funds. Quite often their major expenses, such as a mortgage on the house and the children's living and educational expenses, were behind them. Furthermore, some of the money they once spent on clothes, lunches away from home, and commuting could now be reallocated.

Compared to the academics, proportionately more retirees from business were apt to say their standard of living was *higher* than before retirement. This improvement was largely due to the nature of the incentive early retirement at institution C2. Because retirees under this program received half-pay for four years on top of their earned retirement benefits, their total income in the four years following retirement was usually as good or even better than before.

Although many of the early retirees were concerned about the potential effects of continued inflation; 95% said that, so far, they had been able to live as well or better than they had expected. Compared to retirees in other age groups, those in the 65 to 66 age group were most likely to have underestimated their standard of living after retirement; 44% of these persons found their standard of living higher than expected.

Professional Activity

Early retirement does not necessarily mean an end to gainful professional activity, especially for academics. Sixty-two percent of the early retirees said they had been employed at one time or another during retirement (Table 8). Although a few persons had held full-time jobs, most of those who reported employment had worked part-time or on intermittent or short-term tasks.[23] The retired faculty members were much more likely to have been employed than the retired corporate employees. Only one-third of the latter had been employed since retirement, compared with 72% of the academic retirees. Age also seems to be a deciding factor. All the academics under age 65 had been employed, compared with 56% of those age 65 or older.

Whether a respondent had been employed since retirement also varied by institution, partly because of the average retirement age at each institution and partly because of differing employment regulations for early retirees. Forty-eight percent of the early retirees from institution A2

Table 8 Employment Since Early Retirement

Age at Retirement	Never Employed	Employed Intermittently/ Short-term	Employed Part-time	Employed Full-time	Total
Academics			Percentages		
67–70	50	50	0	0	100 (4)
65–66	43	37	20	0	100 (30)
63–64	0	14	86	0	100 (7)
60–62	0	33	50	17	100 (6)
55–59	0	20	60	20	100 (5)
Subtotal	29	33	35	4	100 (52)
Corporate Employees					
63–64	100	0	0	0	100 (3)
60–62	63	25	0	13	100 (8)
55–59	57	14	29	0	100 (7)
Subtotal	67	17	11	6	100 (18)
Total	39	29	29	4	100 (70)

had been employed, compared with 100% of the retirees from the remaining academic institutions. Besides being the oldest of the retirees (on the average), the early retirees from institution A2 technically were forbidden to accept "gainful employment" while receiving their early-retirement checks from the university. (Many, but not all, of the retired faculty members from institution A2 assumed that this restriction excludes short-term or intermittent consulting activities.) In contrast, the early retirees from institution A3 were generally *required* to work part-time at the university so that their early retirement pension plus their part-time salary would equal the full pension they would have received at the mandatory retirement age. The only employment regulation for early retirees from institution A1 was that they cannot work for the university.

Retired academics in the sciences were more likely to have been employed than those in other fields. Eighty-six percent of the scientists had been employed, compared with 57% of the professors from the humanities. This difference could reflect the relatively greater market-ability of scientific skills, but age at retirement and the nature of the institution left also influence reemployment statistics. Besides being the youngest academics, nearly all the scientists were from either institution A1, where there was no employment restriction, or from institution A3,

where employment was required. Current employment status follows
much the same pattern as employment since retirement. The biggest difference is that only half as many retirees from institution A2 were currently employed.

Seventy-seven percent of the respondents were satisfied with the
amount of time they are working, whether it was part-time, intermit-
tently, or not at all. However, the two respondents currently working
full-time said they would rather be working less. Except for them, satisfaction with the amount of paid work increased slightly with more intensive employment.

Of course, it is possible to stay professionally involved in ways other
than taking a job. One can also carry on independent research and
writing, participate in professional societies, consult without pay, and
perform various volunteer activities related to one's field. If we count
these acitvities as well as employment in one's field, 70% of the early
retirees in this study have been professionally involved at one time or
another during their retirement (Table 9). Again, the percentage is much
higher for the retired faculty members than for the retired corporate

Table 9 Professional Activity Since
Early Retirement

Age at Retirement	Ever Professionally Active?		
	No	Yes	Total
Academics		Percentages	
67–70	0	100	100 (4)
65–66	27	73	100 (30)
63–64	0	100	100 (7)
60–62	0	100	100 (6)
55–59	20	80	100 (5)
Subtotal	17	83	100 (52)
Corporate Employees			
63–64	100	0	100 (3)
60–62	50	50	100 (8)
55–59	71	29	100 (7)
Subtotal	67	33	100 (18)
Total	30	70	100 (70)

employees (83% and 33%, respectively). All but one of the academics who had not been professionally active were age 65 or older when they retired. Finally, although academics in the humanities had a much lower employment rate than academics in other fields, they were comparable to the other academics in overall professional involvement.

General Well-Being and Activity

Asked how happy they were with their present lives compared with how they had felt about their lives in the few years before retirement, only one person (an academic) reported he was less happy. Sixty-one percent of those responding said they were happier than before; 26% said they felt the same; and 11% said they were ambivalent. Virtually the same distribution of answers came from the academics and corporate employees. Many said they were more contented and relaxed because they finally had the freedom to do what they wanted when they wanted to do it. Many were also glad to be away from the tensions and pressures of business or academia.

Well, if you take the last five years before the retirement came up, I was really getting unhappy. I was frustrated. I knew I wasn't making my way the way I should have been making my way in the departmental structure. And I've really been happier since I started my leave, and particularly since I've gotten out here. (A1-4, science)

I think maybe [I'm] a bit more happy because I'm getting more done on the things I'm anxious to get done before I check in. . . . Because of my experience over the years, I feel sort of egotistically that I have a calling to get them done. (A2-5, science)

Much more happy. Less tension, that's the main thing. And no more unnecessary worry about your duties and responsibilities. . . . I used to feel sorry for retired people. I used to think they had been "put on the shelf." Now I go down there and I feel sorry for the ones who still have to do it, still have to publish and cater to the dean and so forth. (A2-8, profession)

More happy. You know, most people won't admit it, but as you get older, it becomes more of a drag to get yourself into a classroom and be vigorous enough to impress the students. (A2-14, profession)

I'm very happy. I didn't like the late Sixties and early Seventies very much. They were very disturbing years in universities everywhere. I didn't like the tremendous enrollments, the complicated bureaucra-

*cies, the period of two to three years of belligerent student atti-
tudes. . . . If I compare right now with those last years, I'm far
more happy (A2-15, science)*

*Happier. Definitely. You know, one of the things that happens to a
married couple when they've both been working is that, when they
retire, they have more time to spend together, which may sound
corny, but it's true. And of course you have your own family, your
own married children, your grandchildren. There's quite a lot to fill
up the days. (A2-24, humanities)*

*I'm much happier now. I've got no problems, other than my bad
back, which I've had for years anyway. When the telephone rings, I
know it's not a problem, somebody calling in sick or something. . . . I'm able to do what I want to do. When I don't want to
do anything, I don't. When I want to do something, I can. (C1-2,
supervisor)*

*Much happier. As I said, I wish I could have enjoyed this way of life
for the last ten years instead of two. . . . I'm very busy, but not as
busy and strained as I was in the last few years with the company.
That was a rat race. It was the nature of the job, the extreme pressure and tension of that job. Seventy or eighty hours a week. Always
a briefcase full of work to do at home on the week-ends. . . . You
can only go at that pace so long until you think, "My god, I got to
get out of it!" (C2-8, corporate executive)*

Approximately one-quarter of the respondents said there was no
change in how happy they were with their lives. Most of these retirees
said they were just as happy as before, but in a different way or for different reasons.

*I'm just as happy as I was before. I'm not frustrated or unhappy. I
liked my work. I enjoyed it very much while I was teaching, but I
don't regret leaving it. . . . I think I feel more relaxed and less under
pressure now, but otherwise my mode of living hasn't changed very
much. (A2-1, profession)*

*I really wasn't discontented when I was working. I was reasonably
happy. I am, of course, more relaxed now; and I can do more of the
things that I wish to do. . . . I'm more relaxed. That's the best way
to describe it. As far as being happier or unhappier, I think that's
about even. (C1-11, engineer)*

Only 12% of the respondents were either ambivalent or less happy with their current lives. The most common complaints of these retirees were feelings of being sidetracked, nonproductive, or bored. Also, several who were genuinely fond of their institution missed being in contact with it and knowing details about its affairs.

Well, there are pluses and minuses. I must say I'm very satisfied with the way my life goes. I spend more time with my wife, which I enjoy. I have a much larger measure of freedom. I couldn't play quite so fast or loose with my time before I retired. On the other hand, I enjoyed what I was doing very much, and I think that in the nature of the case I miss—although not to the extent of making me unhappy about it—I miss the ongoing, day-to-day contact and knowledge of the affairs of the university. I'm very fond of the university, and I miss doing the things which kept me in contact with it. (A3-5, social science)

It does take some getting used to. . . . I'm still not quite adjusted. . . . If you enjoy what you're doing, you put a great deal more into it than you may realize at the time. It can be very absorbing. And when you chop that off, there is a void left, and it is extremely hard to sit on your butt and do nothing. . . . I think the only way you can honestly answer that is that both things are true: there are times when you'd no sooner go back to work than fly, and there are other times when you can become bored and wish you had something more demanding, more stimulating to do. It's a mixed bag. There are periods of ups and downs, and I'm sure that it's the same when you're working. (C2-4, manager)

I miss being in the mainstream. I miss not knowing as much about my corporation as I used to. I'm very business-oriented. . . . I feel somewhat sidetracked, that I've sidetracked myself. On the other hand, the advantages are the things I'm doing that I couldn't do if I were working. (C2-9, manager)

Only a few retirees said they did not have enough interesting and challenging things to do; many, in fact, said they hardly had enough time to accomplish all that they wanted to do. Most were simply devoting more time to interests they had had all their lives. Others had developed entirely new interests.

About one-third of the early retirees had changed residences since they retired. This figure might have been higher if 37% of the early retirees had not been living already in areas considered ideal for retirement—California and Florida, for example. On the other hand, many of the early retirees who remained in the North, especially the academics who stayed near campus, said they would not think of leaving their family, friends, and professional associations behind. The early retirees who did move had various reasons for doing so. Some said they thought it was better psychologically to make a completely fresh start and set new goals for themselves in a new environment. Others moved for a change in climate, either because they or their spouses had a health problem or because they wanted the opportunity for year-round outdoor activity. A few were returning to their original hometowns or joining friends or family.

PREPARATIONS FOR EARLY RETIREMENT

Since few of the interviewees had made long-range plans to retire early, it should not be surprising that a majority of them had not prepared themselves specifically for early retirement financially or in other ways.

More than one-third of the early retirees had made specific financial preparations for early retirement (Table 10). Most frequently, these retirees cited investments and savings as their means of preparation. Of course, that the other retirees had not made financial plans *specifically* for early retirement does not mean they had ignored financial planning altogether. In fact, nine out of ten early retirees mentioned dividends and interest among their current sources of income, although the principal source of income was almost always the retiree's pension.

Thirty-nine percent of the early retirees said they had made specific nonfinancial preparations for early retirement. Most frequently, they mentioned that they had sought a place to relocate or had planned a move; many had made special trips to study retirement communities. Others reported that they had started reducing their work activities—not accepting new graduate students, cleaning out their files, training their successors, refusing new responsibilities, and even going on semiretirement. Still others said they had deliberately developed outside interests and had lined up other activities for after retirement. A few reported preparing themselves and their families psychologically. Two respondents said they had planned to take a long trip immediately after retiring in order to get themselves out of "the work habit." Another respondent

Table 10 Financial Preparations Made Specifically for Early Retirement

Age at Retirement		Financial Preparations					
	None	Investments	Savings	Retaining Annuity from Other Job(s)	Purchase of Supplemental Annuity	Other	Total
			Percentages				
Academics							
67–70	100	0	0	0	0	0	a (4)
65–66	53	37	30	3	17	3	a(30)
63–64	25	0	75	25	0	0	a (4)
60–62	83	17	0	0	0	0	a (6)
55–59	80	20	0	0	0	0	a (5)
Subtotal	61	27	25	4	10	2	a(49)
Corporate Employees							
63–64	100	0	0	0	0	0	a (3)
60–62	75	0	13	0	0	25	a (8)
55–59	43	43	14	0	0	29	a (7)
Subtotal	67	17	11	0	0	22	a(18)
Total	63	24	21	3	7	7	a(67)

Note: MO = 3.

aBecause respondents were able to cite more than one type of preparation, some rows add up to more than 100%.

"experimented" with retirement during his last sabbatical by living in the community he and his wife had chosen for retirement.

Most of the respondents (86%) reported they had not received formal counseling regarding their early retirement decision and the preparations it would require. On the other hand, 93% of those who had not received counseling said they did not feel they needed it. Although many said it might be a good idea for other people, others said they doubted counseling could help anyone.

EVALUATION OF THE ARRANGEMENTS

All but two of the early retirees were either satisfied or very satisfied with the provisions of their early-retirement arrangements. By far the largest number were very satisfied. Indeed, many of the respondents seemed to be enthusiastically in favor of the programs.

I think the arrangement is eminently fair and attractive. . . . I just hope the program becomes larger so that more people can retire early, not only for themselves but also for the benefit of the younger people. (A1-2, science)

This plan was a godsend to me. It gave me the chance to get out early. . . . I think getting the deal that we get is doing pretty well. You can't kick at that. I don't know of any more generous in the nation. I don't know of any other that allows almost five years of coasting at almost the same salary you had while you were there. (A2-21, social science)

I think I was damn lucky. I mean, to have early retirement. . . . One could always wish there were more money, but that would not be realistic. What they're doing now is extremely generous. (A2-23, profession)

I think it's a good idea. It's a tremendous idea. I hope that they propagate this through all the universities. (A3-1, science)

It's awful hard to beat that plan. (C1-12, supervisor)

The special payment program itself is very good and basically quite simple and works very well. (C2-3, manager)

On the other hand, many respondents were reluctant to recommend early retirement to everyone. Since everyone's standards are different, they said, the decision definitely had to be made on one's own. However, they generally praised the voluntary early retirement programs for the added flexibility they offer the individual.

> *It's definitely a matter of individual choice. For some people, early retirement may be disastrous. (A1-2, science)*

> *As I say, it depends on the individual. In my own case, I felt it was very advantageous because it would allow me to do things that I couldn't do otherwise. Of course, every person has different standards, and it wouldn't be right for everyone. I think it's just another alternative in the retirement system that gives people a little more freedom. (A3-2, science)*

> *For me it was an offer I couldn't refuse, but I can understand how many people couldn't accept it. . . . You take some of the people on the clerical staff. Say they make $15,000. Then two years' salary spread out over four years isn't much of a kicker. (C2-7, manager)*

Most of the early retirees seemed to be very realistic about, and sympathetic with, the reasons institutions have for implementing early-retirement programs. The early retirees also seemed to recognize the high costs of some early-retirement options, which the institutions must weigh against their benefits.

> *The dean's attempt to get faculty to retire early to make room at the bottom is a very solid plan, academically and pragmatically. It is very good for the university. (A1-1, science)*

> *I'm really surprised at how generous it is because I have some fairly good ideas of how much this is costing the university out of their academic budget. . . . On the other hand, they don't have to provide me with an office or secretarial services. (A1-4, science)*

> *I think it's a nice deal. Of course, the fringe by-product is that other people can find jobs. For instance, we've increased the number of women in our department. A young woman got my job, for example. (A2-4, social science)*

> *It does have the advantage of substituting younger people more quickly, especially if some of the older faculty members aren't so interested in being active in teaching anymore. . . . Getting younger people onto the faculty is important because often they're the ones with new ideas and certainly with more ambition. (A3-2, science)*

The university profits by getting rid of us old guys, which is realistic. Being able to replace professors who have lost usefulness, saving the big salaries, that's part of the package of this thing. (A3-4, science)

It does cost them a lot of money. They actually only get one-half of the salary savings back. The rest they have to pay into the retirement system. Of course, they still get the other half. I think this is a big advantage to the university. Also, I think an advantage to the university is that, given the physiology of age, most people after 60 or 65 are just not as capable of doing prolonged or intensive work as before. (A3-8, science)

I think a company can only offer as good an early-retirement program as its financial conditions permit. And my own feeling is that a company isn't obliged to keep you forever in the style to which you've been accustomed. (C1-3, manager)

I think the company must have seen the advantages of making early retirement attractive in order to free up positions, get rid of some older people, many of whom are not as productive as they once were. . . . Although the company has done these things which have benefited me, I think it has benefited the company, too. (C2-9, manager)

We asked the interviewees whether, despite their general satisfaction, they felt any changes should be made in the provisions of the arrangements or whether any additional options should be offered.[24] Few respondents had specific changes or alternatives to suggest. In most instances, the changes suggested applied to particular types of arrangements offered by one or more of the institutions. For example, twelve of the twenty-nine retirees from institution A2 felt that the rule forbidding gainful employment during the early-retirement period ought to be rescinded or made more flexible. On the other hand, a number of the other employees from that institution felt that the rule was reasonable, given that they were in effect still receiving university salaries.

Consider another example. At institution C2, the early-retirement arrangement was a lump-sum severance payment paid out over four years. Three of this institution's nine respondents wished they could have had the option of spread-out or deferred payments. They were concerned primarily that the payment boosted them into a higher income-tax bracket for the first four years of retirement, but they also mentioned that the tremendous drop in income after the fourth year could also be a problem. Although inflation seemed to concern a number of the early retirees, only six recommended that full or partial cost-of-living adjustments be included in the early-retirement arrangements.

Five early retirees said they felt the special early-retirement option should be available to a wider range of people—that is, to younger employees and to those with fewer years of service. Also, several of the respondents from institution A2, where the mandatory retirement age was 70, felt the whole retirement system should be redesigned for mandatory retirement and maximum benefits at age 65.

As a group, the early retirees were extremely well satisfied with the administrative handling of their early retirements. However, the respondents from institution A3 seemed to be generally dissatisfied. They complained about their inability to get adequate information; the administrative staff's obvious lack of knowledge about early-retirement benefits, requirements, and procedures; the awkwardness of dealing with the various administrative staffs of departments, their former campus, and the central university; the difficulty of having to deal with both the retirement system and the academic structure; the profusion of confusing written agreements; delays in the processing of retirement papers; and disagreements or misunderstandings over interpretation of individual contracts and of university policy. In contrast, the other retirees made a point of saying that their institutions handled early retirements very smoothly and very routinely, with a minimum of paperwork and much concern that the retiree fully understand the agreement.

THE POTENTIAL EARLY RETIREES

If induced early retirement is to be effective, then it must appeal to the less-productive faculty members. Few institutions would want to spend money on a program that caused their most effective teachers and researchers to leave. Therefore, most of the incentive early-retirement schemes in both business and academia are intended to encourage marginal employees to terminate early. Given the proper incentives, will the least-productive and most disaffected academics agree to retire early?

In the University of California study, salary levels and publication rates—two commonly accepted measures of academic achievement—were negatively associated with a willingness to retire earlier than originally planned. That is, controlling for age and length of service, the academics who say they might retire earlier than they now anticipate if conditions were right tend to have relatively low salaries and fewer publications.[25]

Using national data to study the possible effect of abolishing mandatory retirement, Ladd, Lipset, and Palmer obtained similar findings. Using measures that included total number of articles published, publications during the last two years, interest in research as opposed to teaching, volume of research funding, and quality of institution, they found "an exceptionally strong correlation between a vigorous research commitment and a commitment to late retirement."[26] The least-productive academics and those with fewer opportunities for scholarly and professional activities outside their teaching appointment were more interested in retiring early.

The incentive early-retirement programs we investigated seemed to attract those academics who, for a variety of reasons, might be considered the best candidates for early retirement.

1. Forty percent of the retiring academics said they had lost interest in or had become dissatisfied with their work, or else felt the pressures of working were too great.

2. Twenty-one percent had health problems or disabilities.

3. Fifteen percent said they were dissatisfied with their own performance.

4. Twelve percent said they were dissatisfied with or could not adapt to a changing administration or the academic focus of their departments or universities.

Overall, 56% of the academics mentioned at least one of these reasons for retiring early, any one of which could have an adverse effect on their productivity and effectiveness. Other factors (such as cost) must be weighed when assessing the benefits of early-retirement programs to a university, but it is clear that early-retirement allows some faculty members a graceful exit. It certainly benefited the persons we interviewed. Almost all the early retirees were satisfied with their decision. Moreover, a majority said they were happier than they were before retirement; and most said that retirement had had no negative effect on their standard of living.

NOTES

1. Part of this chapter appeared in Diane Kell and Carl Vernon Patton, "Reaction to Induced Early Retirement," *The Gerontologist* 18, no. 2

(April 1978), pp. 173-179. Permission to reprint granted by the Gerontological Society.

2. Alan R. Rowe, "Scientists in Retirement," *Journal of Gerontology* 28, no. 3 (July 1973): 345-350; and Alan R. Rowe, "Retired Academics and Research Activity," *Journal of Gerontology* 31, no. 4 (July 1976): 456-461.

3. Mark H. Ingrahm, *My Purpose Holds: Reactions and Experiences in Retirement of TIAA—CREF Annuitants* (New York: Teachers Insurance and Annuity Association—College Retirement Equities Fund, 1974); Gordon F. Streib and Clement J. Schneider, *Retirement in American Society: Impact and Practice* (Ithaca, New York: Cornell University Press, 1971); Carl Vernon Patton, "Early Retirement as a Policy for a 'Steady-State' University," Ph.D. dissertation, School of Public Policy (Berkeley: University of California, 1976); and James Peterson and Ann Morey, "Factors Related to Faculty Morale and Satisfaction During Retirement," mimeo. (Los Angeles: University of Southern California, Office of Institutional Studies, 1976).

4. Everett Carll Ladd, Jr., Seymour Martin Lipset, and David D. Palmer, "The American Professoriate: The Issue of Mandatory Retirement," mimeo.,University of Connecticut, School of Business Administration (Storrs, Conn.: 1977). Summarized as Everett Carll Ladd, Jr., and Seymour Martin Lipset, "Many Professors Would Postpone Retirement if Law Were Changed (The Ladd-Lipset Faculty Survey)" *Chronicle of Higher Education,* 7 November 1977, pp. 7-8; and Patton, "Early Retirement."

5. Patton, "Early Retirement"; Peterson and Morey, "Faculty Morale and Satisfaction"; and James M. Mulanaphy, *1972-73 Survey of Retired TIAA—CREF Annuitants* (New York: Teachers Insurance and Annuity Association—College Retirement Equities Fund, 1974).

6. Richard E. Barfield and James N. Morgan, "Trends in Satisfaction with Retirement," *The Gerontologist* 18, no. 1 (February 1978): pp. 19-23; and Walter F. Chatfield, "Economic and Sociological Factors Influencing Life Satisfaction Among the Aged," *Journal of Gerontology* 32, no. 5 (September 1977): 593-599; and Reed Larson, "Thirty Years of Research on the Subjective Well-Being of Older Americans," *Journal of Gerontology* 33, no. 1 (January 1978): 101-125.

7. Robert C. Atchley, "Disengagement Among Professors," *Journal of Gerontology* 26, no. 4 (October 1971): 476-480.

8. Mulanaphy, *1972-73 Survey;* Patton, "Early Retirement"; Peterson and Morey, "Faculty Morale and Satisfaction;" and Robert B. Snow and

Robert J. Havighurst, "Life Style Types and Patterns of Retirement of Educators," *The Gerontologist* 17, no. 6 (December 1977): pp. 545–552.

9. Paul Roman and Philip Taietz, "Organizational Structure and Disengagement: The Emeritus Professor," *The Gerontologist* 7, no. 3 (September 1967): 147–152.

10. Leonard Gernant, "A Study of 814 Retired Professors in Michigan," mimeo. (Kalamazoo, Michigan: Western Michigan University, 1971), p. 37.

11. Atchley, "Disengagement"; Ingrahm, *My Purpose Holds;* and Patton, "Early Retirement."

12. Rowe, "Retired Academics and Research Activity," p. 459. In an earlier study, Rowe found 33% of retired academic scientists reemployed, most in teaching or research. See Rowe, "Scientists in Retirement," p. 347.

13. Mulanaphy, *1972–73 Survey,* p. 68.

14. Patton, "Early Retirement."

15. Patton, "Early Retirement." Summarized in part as Carl Vernon Patton, "Early Retirement in Academia: Making the Decision," *The Gerontologist* 17, no. 4 (August 1977): 347–354.

16. Peterson and Morey, "Faculty Morale and Satisfaction," p. 31.

17. Ladd, Lipset, and Palmer, "The American Professoriate."

18. Diane Kell conducted most of the interviews reported in this chapter and drafted the analysis on which this part of the chapter is based.

19. Patton, "Early Retirement."

20. In this vein, eight of the respondents from institution A3 were asked during an earlier study whether they had planned to retire when they did. Six of the seven who responded said they retired sooner than they had planned.

21. Note that this was an open-ended, rather than multiple-choice, question. Individual respondents mentioned anywhere from one to five reasons for retiring early. No more than three answers per respondent were included in the analysis in order to eliminate minor reasons for retiring. This adjustment had minimal effect on the rank order of the reasons across respondents.

22. This was an open-ended, rather than multiple-choice, question. Also, there was no double-counting across categories.

23. To be classified as employment, an activity had to have been remunerated with more than a token honorarium or paid expenses. A "full-time" activity had to have been scheduled for five full days per week every week and

must have continued for thirty days or more. A "part-time" activity, although it could require less than five days per week, must also have been weekly and continued for thirty days or more. "Intermittent/short-term" activities include all those which were not weekly or were less than thirty days in length. They also include all special projects and *ad hoc* tasks, whether or not they meet other full-time and part-time criteria. There is no double counting. "Full-time" subsumes persons who had worked both full-time and in one of the other categories, and "part-time" subsumes those who had worked both part-time and on intermittent, short-term tasks.

24. This was an open-ended, rather than multiple-choice, question.

25. Patton, "Early Retirement," pp. 224–227.

26. Ladd, Lipset, and Palmer, "The American Professoriate," p. 15.

4

Fiscal Implications of Early Retirement

An institution considering an incentive early-retirement scheme must analyze the effect of alternative options on its faculty. This chapter discusses the basic factors that should be included in such an analysis. Although each institution must compute the costs and benefits of alternative schemes using its own data, the following pages indicate the relative effectiveness of a variety of short-run options. Whether these options can be implemented will depend on forthcoming legislation and rule-making. Legal counsel should certainly be obtained by any institution which considers the adoption of one of these options.

When academic institutions initially considered adopting incentive early-retirement plans, some of them overestimated their expected savings. Their errors derived from several sources, including: (1) underestimating supplemental payments, (2) assuming that faculty members who retired early would not need to be replaced, (3) underestimating the salaries that would have to be paid replacement employees, and (4) failing to include associated costs, such as those of recruiting new employees. Although these problems can be avoided, the precise costs of any alternative remain somewhat difficult to estimate and will depend on local decisions. For example, an institution must decide how large a supplement is required to encourage an employee to retire early. Must 100% of salary be paid the employee, or will 75% be enough? The institution must also decide whether cost-of-living adjustments must be provided. Will the supplement be geared to the particular employee's salary, or might it be related to the median salary of his age and service cohort?

The costs and benefits for the institution will also depend on the salary being paid the potential early retiree, on either the number of years service credit (defined-benefit plans) or the amount accumulated in his pension account (defined-contribution plans),[1] on expected salary increases, and on other factors.

ILLUSTRATION OF COST CALCULATIONS

To illustrate the factors that should be considered, we calculated costs for several early-retirement options using data drawn from one of the case institutions and assuming mandatory retirement at age 67. These examples depict situations in which a supplemental payment or a supplemental annuity is financed over several years. A lump-sum severance payment would be made in a different manner, most likely as a single payment from institutional revenues. Several of the most promising options discussed in chapter 1 are analyzed below.

Option 1: Full-Salary Early Annuity. The early retiree begins to draw his regular early-retirement annuity and also is paid the difference between his early annuity and his former salary. The institution purchases a supplemental annuity to go into effect at the mandatory retirement age, thus assuring the early retiree an income at that time equal to his projected mandatory-age annuity. This is Alternative 1 in chapter 1.

Option 2: Individual-Based Early Annuity. The early retiree receives his regular early-retirement annuity plus a supplemental annuity that raises his total retirement income up to what he would have received if he had retired at the mandatory retirement age. This is Alternative 3 in chapter 1.

Option 3: Group-Based Early Annuity. Under this option, the supplement is equal to the difference between the retiree's own early-retirement annuity and the median mandatory-age annuity for his age and service group. This is Alternative 4 in chapter 1.

Option 4: Individual-Based Early Annuity with Partial Employment. In this case, the early retiree receives his early-retirement annuity and is provided part-time employment until he reaches the mandatory retirement age. His income then equals his preretirement salary. At mandatory retirement, the early retiree begins to receive a supplemental annuity, which, when combined with his early-retirement annuity, yields a pension the size of his projected mandatory-age annuity. This is Alternative 5 in chapter 1.

Options 5 and 6: Continued Annuity Contributions. These two options require the early retiree to defer all retirement benefits until the mandatory retirement age. Between retirement and the time he reaches the mandatory retirement age, the institution either continues payments to his annuity fund *or* purchases him a supplemental annuity. At the mandatory retirement age, his total annuity is equal to what he would have received had he remained employed. These options are variations on Alternative 7 in chapter 1.

To estimate the costs and benefits of the early-retirement alternatives, we calculated both mandatory-age annuity benefits and early-retirement annuity benefits for potential retirees. We took age 67 as our mandatory retirement age since it approximates the average age at which university employees are required to retire. The present mean salary of every age-service cohort was converted to an expected salary at age 67 by increasing it 2% per year (assuming that 2% is the average annual real salary increase).[2] The single life annuity (SLA) that would be received if the employee retired at age 67 is calculated from the benefits schedule of one of our case institutions. We derived the SLA that would be received if the employee retired at his present age from the same source.

Also calculated is the difference between the early-retirement annuity and the annuity for retirement at age 67. This figure is the Supplemental SLA (SSLA) required to make the early retiree's pension equal to what is received by a person who retires at age 67. The total value of the SSLA is determined from the actuarial table. Its present value is found by discounting at 6%. Since it is desirable to purchase the supplemental annuity on a level basis (the same dollar payment during each year until the employee reaches age 67), the level annual cost of the SSLA is calculated by dividing the present value of the SSLA by its annuity value (a factor related to the time period during which the annuity will be purchased).

To calculate the costs of the group-based early annuity, each age-service cohort is divided into three subgroups representing the high-third, middle-third, and low-third wage earners. Then the value of the SSLA for members of each subgroup is calculated, based on the *median* salary for the entire age-service cohort.

The results of these calculations give us the basis for the cost analysis. For each alternative we determined: (1) the yearly supplement required to meet the plan's salary objectives, (2) the total annual cost of retiring an average employee, (3) the balance of the retired employee's salary line freed for hiring a new employee, (4) the salary for a full-time equivalent (FTE) assistant professorship that the freed salary line will finance until the year the early retiree reaches age 67, and (5) the annual income of the early retiree until age 67, when he begins to draw the single life annuity he would have received had he retired at that age.

We describe the effects of each option on employees retiring at age 62 (the lowest age at which social-security benefits may be received), age 60, age 55, and age 50. Differences caused by varying the years of service credit from seventeen to thirty-two years for the oldest age group, and from ten to twenty years for the youngest age group, are illustrated. Under the group-based annuity, the supplemental pension is calculated for persons in the high-third, middle-third, and low-third salary groups. In this case, the consequences are depicted for fewer service credit groups in order to keep the illustration manageable.

In a previous analysis, it was found that it is expensive to retire an employee less than 55 years of age or with less than ten years of service credit.[3] Further, in most retirement systems, 55 is the earliest permissible retirement age. However, for illustration, we include employees 50 years of age with at least ten years of service credit. In practice, persons with less than ten years service credit are usually not eligible for supplemental early-retirement benefits. Providing supplemental benefits to a retiree under age 55 with less than ten years of service credit does not free sufficient funds for a replacement employee. However, in some age and service cohorts the retirement of an employee would free more than enough money to hire a replacement faculty member. For example, a 62-year-old faculty member with seventeen years of service could be retired on an individual-based early annuity that would free funds enough to hire a young faculty member. It is assumed that assistant professors would be hired at an average starting salary of $15,000 per nine-month academic year.

Cost computations are based on faculty salary, age, and service-credit data from one of our case institutions. The estimates are based on the current actuarial tables and benefit formulas in use at that institution.[4] Calculations are performed in present-value terms, using a 6% discount rate.[5] For ease of illustration, this analysis is performed for male faculty members only. Moreover, there are currently few older female professors, and in the future pension benefits may well be based upon unisex actuarial tables.

When an employee retires early, his early-retirement benefit is the actuarial equivalent of the normal retirement benefit. That is, the actuarial tables reflect the fact that the retirement pension must be paid over a longer period and is based on a lower level of contributions. When special early-retirement benefits are added to the normal early-retirement pension, their cost must be either absorbed by increased contributions or paid for through funds budgeted by the organization. The second approach is used here because it is immediately available to institutions and it does not affect the contribution rates of other employees.

Since it is next to impossible to predict inflation rates, inflation has been excluded from the calculations of the retiree's projected salary at age 67. The calculations are carried out in real-dollar terms, and the 2% increase assumed for each year between the early-retirement and mandatory-retirement ages represents a real increase in income. However, it could be assumed that the early retiree will receive, during the early-retirement period, cost-of-living adjustments on his pension and supplement equal to the inflation rate that would have been assigned to his budget line had he remained employed. This assumption appears reasonable, for this budget line is used to finance both the early retiree's supplement and his replacement's salary during the early-retirement period. After the early retiree reaches the mandatory retirement age, however, his annuity would be adjusted at the rate in effect for all members of his retirement system—if, in fact, annuitants are provided cost-of-living adjustments.

No matter what the option, the early retiree might suffer a reduction in eventual social-security income unless he reemploys. This reduction could be substantial for people retiring a decade or more early. The calculations for the continued annuity payments option assume that a person electing this option would move to other employment and continue to pay into social security; therefore, they do not assume continued institutional contributions to social security.

Results of the Calculations

Calculations for each option appear in Tables 11 through 16. All tables are read in a similar manner. In Table 11, for example, the present age, years of service credit, and mean salary for each age-service cohort are listed. Placing these data into a benefits formula yields the single life annuity to which an average-salaried employee in each age-service cohort would be entitled if he retired early. (See column 4.) In order to determine the single life annuity that the average-salaried employee

Table 11 Full-Salary Early Annuity

1	2	3	4	5	6	7	8	9	10
Current Age	Years Service Credit Now	Present Mean Salary for Age-Service Cohort	Single Life Annuity (SLA) Now	Expected Salary at 67, 2%/Year Real Increase	Single Life Annuity at 67	Supplemental SLA Required at 67 (SSLA) [6–4]	Value of SSLA at 67 [7×9,384]	Present Value of SSLA at 6% Discount	Level Annual Cost of SSLA [9÷Annuity Value]
								(.7473)	(4.4651)
62	32	$32,500	$22,880	$35,750	$28,600	$5,720	$53,676	$40,112	$8,984
62	27	30,400	18,058	33,440	24,612	6,554	61,501	45,960	10,293
62	22	29,500	14,181	32,450	20,152	5,970	56,027	41,869	9,377
62	17	33,500	12,529	36,850	18,646	6,117	57,402	42,897	9,607
								(.6651)	(5.9173)
60	30	30,200	18,120	34,730	27,784	9,664	90,687	60,315	10,193
60	25	28,600	14,300	32,890	24,207	9,907	92,967	61,832	10,449
60	20	26,700	10,680	30,705	19,067	8,387	78,704	52,346	8,846
60	15	26,400	7,920	30,360	15,362	7,442	69,836	46,448	7,850
								(.4970)	(8.8869)
55	25	29,100	10,193	36,957	29,566	19,373	181,796	90,353	10,167
55	20	29,000	8,700	36,830	27,107	18,407	172,731	85,847	9,660
55	15	25,600	5,760	32,512	20,190	14,430	135,411	67,299	7,573
55	10	25,000	3,750	31,750	16,066	12,316	115,573	57,440	6,463
								(.3713)	(11.1060)
50	20	29,200	5,840	40,880	32,704	26,864	252,092	93,602	8,428
50	15	26,400	3,960	36,960	27,202	23,242	218,103	80,982	7,292
50	10	25,000	2,500	35,000	21,735	19,235	180,501	67,020	6,035

92

Table 11 Continued

11 Supplement Required to Match Present Salary [3-4]	12 Annual Total Required to Retire Employee [10+11]	13 Balance of Budget Line Released [3-12]	14 FTE Assistant Professor at $15,000 per ER for Duration	15 Total Annual Incentive ER (IER) Income [3]	16 IER as a Percentage of Current Salary [15÷3]	17 IER as a Percentage of Regular ER Annuity [15÷4]	18 IER as a Percentage of Mandatory R Annuity [15÷6]
$9,620	$18,603	$13,897	.93	$32,500	100	142	114
12,342	21,326	9,074	.60	30,400	100	168	124
15,319	24,696	4,804	.32	29,500	100	208	146
20,971	30,038	3,462	.23	33,500	100	267	180
12,080	22,273	7,927	.53	30,200	100	167	108
14,300	24,749	3,851	.26	28,600	100	200	118
16,020	24,866	1,834	.12	26,700	100	250	140
18,480	26,330	70	.01	26,400	100	333	172
18,907	29,074	26	< .01	29,100	100	285	98
20,300	29,960	-960	*	29,000	100	333	107
19,840	27,413	-1,813	*	25,600	100	444	127
21,250	27,713	-2,713	*	25,000	100	667	156
23,360	31,788	-2,588	*	29,200	100	500	89
22,440	29,732	-3,332	*	26,400	100	667	97
22,500	28,535	-3,535	*	25,000	100	1000	115

*Negative Value

would receive if he retired at the mandatory age, it is necessary to estimate his expected salary at age 67. This figure, found in column 5, is produced by increasing the current mean salary by 2% per year until age 67. Column 6 lists the single life annuity that the retiree at age 67 would receive. This figure is calculated from the benefits formula and assumes that the employee reached age 67, received the expected salary increases, and accumulated a service credit equal to what he achieved up to early retirement plus the number of years between his early and mandatory retirement.

In column 7, the difference between the mandatory-age annuity and the early annuity is reported. This is the supplemental annuity required at age 67. Since the supplement is purchased before the mandatory retirement age, its present value must be determined. First, the supplement is multiplied by a factor (9.384) which produces the value of the supplement at the mandatory retirement age (column 8). (The "value" of the supplement is the total amount of supplemental payments the employee can expect to receive from the time he reaches the mandatory retirement age until his death, which the actuarial tables assume to average 9.384 years later.) Next, the values in column 8 are discounted at 6% per year for the period from now until the employee reaches the mandatory retirement age. (For example, a dollar to be received five years from now, assuming a 6% discount rate, would be worth $0.7473 today. One to be received seven years from now would be worth $0.6651.) The present value of the supplemental annuity at age 67 is reported in column 9.

Assuming that the supplemental annuity will be purchased with funds from the retiring employee's salary line, it would be convenient to pay for the annuity in equal annual payments. Thus, the level annual cost of the supplement is computed in column 10. This figure is found by dividing the present value of the supplemental annuity at age 67 by the annuity value. (The "annuity value" describes the present worth of one dollar per year, from now until the early retiree's mandatory retirement age. For example, one dollar each year for the next five years discounted at 6% would equal $4.4651 today.)

Columns 1 through 10 provide, then, the basic data needed to determine the fiscal impact of the option. In columns 11 through 18, the annual amounts needed to retire one employee and the amount of funds his early retirement releases are reported. Also, the incentive early-retirement annuity is expressed as a percentage of current salary, as a percentage of the early retiree's annuity, and as a percentage of his mandatory-age annuity.

The key columns to examine are: column 12, the annual total amount required to retire the average-salaried employee; column 13, the funds released by each early retirement for the mean salary in a given age and service cohort; column 14, the proportion of an assistant professor's salary paid for by savings from each early retiree; column 16, the early-retirement income as a percentage of current salary; column 17, the early-retirement income as a percentage of the regular early-retirement annuity; and column 18, the early-retirement income as a percentage of the mandatory-age annuity. Columns 12, 13, and 14 are of central concern to the institution; columns 16, 17, and 18 are of special interest to the potential early retiree.

Table 12, "Individual-Based Early Annuity," shows an option designed to provide an early-retirement pension equal to the pension the early retiree would have received had he remained employed until the mandatory age and had he received annual real salary increases of 2%. The table lists the annuity the employee would receive if he retired today without a supplement (column 4) and the expected annuity at age 67 (column 6). The supplement is shown in column 7, and the present value of the supplement at age 67 is shown in column 9. Columns 13 and 14 deal with the amounts released and the proportion of an assistant professor's salary that could be financed by one early retirement at each of the various age and service levels. Of most interest to the potential early retiree are columns 16, 17, and 18, which compare the incentive early-retirement income with the retiree's current salary, with his regular early-retirement annuity, and with his expected mandatory-age annuity.

Table 13, "Group-Based Early Annuity," lists figures based not on the early retiree's projected benefits but on the median projected benefits of his age and service cohort. Except for being computed for high-, middle-, and low-income groups, this table is read in the same way as Tables 11 and 12.

Table 14, "Individual-Based Early Annuity with Partial Employment," shows the outcome of an option that provides the supplement to the regular early-retirement annuity through part-time employment (up to 49% of full-time). As with the other options, a supplemental annuity is purchased to make up the difference between the early-retirement annuity and the mandatory-age annuity, to go into effect at the mandatory age. The table is read in the same way as the earlier tables.

Schemes more financially attractive to the institution (and thus less financially attractive to the employee) are illustrated in Table 15, "Supplemental Annuity to Continue Annuity Contributions until Age

Table 12 Individual-Based Early Annuity

1	2	3	4	5	6	7	8	9	10
Current Age	Years Service Credit Now	Present Mean Salary for Age-Service Cohort	Single Life Annuity (SLA) Now	Expected Salary at 67, 2%/Year Real Increase	Single Life Annuity at 67	Supplemental SLA Required at 67 (SSLA) [6−4]	Value of SSLA at 67 [7×9.384]	Present Value of SSLA at 6% Discount	Level Annual Cost of SSLA [9÷Annuity Value]
62	32	$32,500	$22,880	$35,750	$28,600	$5,720	$53,676	(.7473) $40,112	(4.4651) $8,984
62	27	30,400	18,058	33,440	24,612	6,554	61,501	45,960	10,293
62	22	29,500	14,181	32,450	20,152	5,970	56,027	41,869	9,377
62	17	33,500	12,529	36,850	18,646	6,117	57,402	42,897	9,607
60	30	30,200	18,120	34,730	27,784	9,664	90,687	(.6651) 60,315	(5.9173) 10,193
60	25	28,600	14,300	32,890	24,207	9,907	92,967	61,832	10,449
60	20	26,700	10,680	30,705	19,067	8,387	78,704	52,346	8,846
60	15	26,400	7,920	30,360	15,362	7,442	69,836	46,448	7,850
55	25	29,100	10,193	36,957	29,566	19,373	181,796	(.4970) 90,353	(8.8869) 10,167
55	20	29,000	8,700	36,830	27,107	18,407	172,731	85,847	9,660
55	15	25,600	5,760	32,512	20,190	14,430	135,411	67,299	7,573
55	10	25,000	3,750	31,750	16,066	12,316	115,573	57,440	6,463
50	20	29,200	5,840	40,880	32,704	26,864	252,092	(.3713) 93,602	(11.1060) 8,428
50	15	26,400	3,960	36,960	27,202	23,242	218,103	80,982	7,292
50	10	25,000	2,500	35,000	21,735	19,235	180,501	67,020	6,035

Table 12 Continued

11 Additional Compensation (Age 67 Annuity Minus SLA Now) [6-4]	12 Annual Total Required to Retire Employee [10+11]	13 Balance of Budget Line Released [3-12]	14 FTE Assistant Professor at $15,000 per ER for Duration	15 Total Annual Incentive ER (IER) Income [4+11]	16 IER as a Percentage of Current Salary [15÷3]	17 IER as a Percentage of Regular ER Annuity [15÷4]	18 IER as a Percentage of Mandatory R Annuity [15÷6]
$5,720	$14,704	$17,796	1.19	$28,600	88	125	100
6,554	16,847	13,553	.90	24,612	81	136	100
5,970	15,347	14,153	.94	20,152	68	142	100
6,117	15,724	17,776	1.18	18,646	55	149	100
9,664	19,857	10,343	.69	27,784	92	153	100
9,907	20,356	8,224	.55	24,207	85	169	100
8,387	17,233	9,467	.63	19,067	71	179	100
7,442	15,292	11,108	.74	15,362	58	194	100
19,373	29,540	-440	*	29,566	102	290	100
18,407	28,067	933	.06	27,107	93	312	100
14,430	22,003	3,597	.24	20,190	79	351	100
12,316	18,779	6,221	.42	16,066	64	428	100
26,864	35,292	-6,092	*	32,704	112	560	100
23,242	30,534	-4,134	*	27,202	103	687	100
19,235	25,270	-270	*	21,735	87	870	100

*Negative Value

97

Table 13 Group-Based Early Annuity

1	2	3	4	5	6	7	8	9	10	11
Current Age	Salary Group[a]	Years Service Credit Now	Present Median Salary for Age-Service Cohort	Own Single Life Annuity (SLA) Now	Own Salary at 67, 2%/Year Real Increase	Own Single Life Annuity at 67	Supplemental SLA Required at 67 (SSLA) [7 Median-5]	Value of SSLA at 67 [8 × 9.384]	Present Value of SSLA at 6% Discount	Level Annual Cost of SSLA [10 ÷ Annuity Value]
									(.7473)	(4.4651)
62	H	32	$38,500	$27,104	$42,350	$33,880	$-1,134	0	0	0
62	M	32	29,500	20,768	32,450	25,960	5,192	$48,722	$36,410	$8,154
62	L	32	26,500	18,656	29,150	23,320	7,304	68,541	51,221	11,471
62	H	27	33,500	19,899	36,850	27,121	3,984	37,386	27,939	6,257
62	M	27	29,500	17,523	32,450	23,883	6,360	59,682	44,600	9,989
62	L	27	26,500	15,741	29,150	21,454	8,142	76,405	57,097	12,787
62	H	22	32,000	15,488	35,200	21,859	4,664	43,767	32,707	7,325
62	M	22	29,500	14,278	32,450	20,152	5,874	55,122	41,193	9,226
62	L	22	26,000	12,584	28,600	17,761	7,568	71,018	53,072	11,886
62	H	17	38,500	14,399	42,350	21,429	4,247	39,854	29,783	6,670
62	M	17	33,500	12,529	36,850	18,646	6,117	57,402	42,897	9,607
62	L	17	23,500	8,789	25,850	13,080	9,857	92,498	69,124	15,481
									(.6651)	(5.9173)

Table 13 Continued

1	2	3	4	5	6	7	8	9	10	11
Current Age	Salary Group[a]	Years Service Credit Now	Present Median Salary for Age-Service Cohort	Own Single Life Annuity (SLA) Now	Own Salary at 67, 2%/Year Real Increase	Own Single Life Annuity at 67	Supplemental SLA Required at 67 (SSLA) [7 Median-5]	Value of SSLA at 67 [8 × 9.384]	Present Value of SSLA at 6% Discount	Level Annual Cost of SSLA [10 ÷ Annuity Value]
60	H	30	34,000	20,400	39,100	31,280	3,980	37,348	24,841	4,198
60	M	30	26,500	15,900	30,475	24,380	8,480	79,576	52,926	8,944
60	L	30	24,500	14,700	28,175	22,540	9,680	90,837	60,416	10,210
60	H	25	32,500	16,250	37,375	27,508	8,126	76,254	50,717	8,571
60	M	25	28,800	14,400	33,120	24,376	9,976	93,614	62,263	10,522
60	L	25	25,400	12,700	29,210	21,499	11,676	109,568	72,874	12,315
60	H	20	35,200	14,080	40,480	25,138	5,916	55,516	36,924	6,240
60	M	20	28,000	11,200	32,200	19,996	8,796	82,542	54,899	9,278
60	L	20	22,500	9,000	25,875	16,068	10,996	103,187	68,630	11,598
									(.4970)	(8.8869)
55	H	20	38,400	11,520	48,768	35,893	14,185	133,112	66,157	7,444
55	M	20	27,500	8,250	34,925	25,705	17,455	163,798	81,408	9,160
55	L	20	21,500	6,450	27,305	20,096	19,255	180,689	89,802	10,105
									(.3713)	(11.1060)
50	H	20	37,300	7,460	52,220	41,776	26,476	248,451	92,250	8,306
50	M	20	30,300	6,060	42,420	33,936	27,876	261,588	97,128	8,746
50	L	20	20,300	4,060	28,420	22,736	29,876	280,356	104,096	9,373

[a]H = high-third, M = mid-third, L = low-third salary group.

99

Table 13 Continued

12	13	14	15	16	17	18	19
Additional Compensation [Age 67 Median SLA Minus SLA Now]	Annual Total Required to Retire Employee [11 + 12]	Balance of Budget Line Released [4 − 13]	FTE Assistant Professor at $15,000 per ER for Duration	Total Annual Incentive ER (IER) Income [7 Median]	IER as a Percentage of Current Salary [16 ÷ 4]	IER as a Percentage of Regular ER Annuity [16 ÷ 5]	IER as a Percentage of Mandatory R Annuity [16 ÷ 7]
$−1,134	0	$38,500	2.57	$27,104[a]	70	100	80
5,192	$13,346	16,154	1.08	25,960	88	125	100
7,304	18,775	7,725	.52	25,960	98	139	111
3,984	10,241	23,259	1.55	23,883	71	120	88
6,360	16,349	13,151	.88	23,883	81	136	100
8,142	20,929	5,571	.37	23,883	90	152	111
4,664	11,989	20,011	1.33	20,152	63	130	92
5,874	15,100	14,400	.96	20,152	68	141	100
7,568	19,451	6,546	.44	20,152	78	160	113
4,247	10,917	27,583	1.84	18,646	48	129	87
6,117	15,724	17,776	1.19	18,646	56	149	100
9,857	25,338	−1,838	*	18,646	79	212	143

Table 13 *Continued*

12	13	14	15	16	17	18	19
Additional Compensation [Age 67 Median SLA Minus SLA Now]	Annual Total Required to Retire Employee [11 + 12]	Balance of Budget Line Released [4 − 13]	FTE Assistant Professor at $15,000 per ER for Duration	Total Annual Incentive ER (IER) Income [7 Median]	IER as a Percentage of Current Salary [16 ÷ 4]	IER as a Percentage of Regular ER Annuity [16 ÷ 5]	IER as a Percentage of Mandatory R Annuity [16 ÷ 7]
3,980	8,178	25,822	1.72	24,380	72	120	78
8,480	17,424	9,076	.61	24,380	92	153	100
9,680	19,890	4,610	.31	24,380	99	166	108
8,126	16,697	15,803	1.05	24,376	75	150	89
9,976	20,498	8,302	.55	24,376	85	169	100
11,676	23,991	1,409	.09	24,376	96	192	113
5,916	12,156	23,044	1.54	19,996	57	142	80
8,796	18,074	9,926	.66	19,996	71	179	100
10,996	22,594	−94	*	19,996	89	222	124
14,185	21,629	16,771	1.12	25,705	67	223	72
17,455	26,615	885	.06	25,705	93	312	100
19,255	29,360	−7,860	*	25,705	120	399	130
26,476	34,782	2,518	.17	33,936	91	455	81
27,876	36,622	−6,322	*	33,936	112	560	100
29,876	39,249	−18,949	*	33,936	167	836	149

[a] Presumably, these persons could not be given incentive early annuities less than their normal early-retirement annuities.

*Negative Value

Table 14 Individual-Based Early Annuity with Partial Employment

1	2	3	4	5	6	7	8	9	10
Current Age	Years Service Credit Now	Present Mean Salary for Age-Service Cohort	Single Life Annuity (SLA) Now	Expected Salary at 67, 2%/Year Real Increase	Single Life Annuity at 67	Supplemental SLA Required at 67 (SSLA) [6−4]	Value of SSLA at 67 [7×9.384]	Present Value of SSLA at 6% Discount	Level Annual Cost of SSLA [9÷Annuity Value]
								(.7473)	(4.4651)
62	32	$32,500	$22,880	$35,750	$28,600	$5,720	$53,676	$40,112	$8,984
62	27	30,400	18,058	33,440	24,612	6,554	61,501	45,960	10,293
62	22	29,500	14,181	32,450	20,152	5,970	56,027	41,869	9,377
62	17	33,500	12,529	36,850	18,646	6,117	57,402	42,897	9,607
								(.6651)	(5.9173)
60	30	30,200	18,120	34,730	27,784	9,664	90,687	60,315	10,193
60	25	28,600	14,300	32,890	24,207	9,907	92,967	61,832	10,449
60	20	26,700	10,680	30,705	19,067	8,387	78,704	52,346	8,846
60	15	26,400	7,920	30,360	15,362	7,442	69,836	46,448	7,850
								(.4970)	(8.8869)
55	25	29,100	10,193	36,957	29,566	19,373	181,796	90,353	10,167
55	20	29,000	8,700	36,830	27,107	18,407	172,731	85,847	9,660
55	15	25,600	5,760	32,512	20,190	14,430	135,411	67,299	7,573
55	10	25,000	3,750	31,750	16,066	12,316	115,573	57,440	6,463
								(.3713)	(11.1060)
50	20	29,200	5,840	40,880	32,704	26,864	252,092	93,602	8,428
50	15	26,400	3,960	36,960	27,202	23,242	218,103	80,982	7,292
50	10	25,000	2,500	35,000	21,735	19,235	180,501	67,020	6,035

Table 14 *Continued*

11 Additional Compensation [49% Salary or Current Salary Minus Annuity]	12 Annual Total Required to Retire Employee [10+11]	13 Balance of Budget Line Released [3-12]	14 FTE Assistant Professor at $15,000 per ER for Duration	15 Total Annual Incentive ER (IER) Income [4+11]	16 IER as a Percentage of Current Salary [15÷3]	17 IER as a Percentage of Regular ER Annuity [15÷4]	18 IER as a Percentage of Mandatory R Annuity [15÷6]
$9,620	$18,604	$13,896	.93	$32,500	100	142	114
12,342	22,635	7,765	.52	30,400	100	168	124
14,455	23,832	5,668	.38	28,636	97	202	142
16,415	26,022	7,478	.50	28,944	86	231	155
12,080	22,273	7,927	.53	30,200	100	167	109
14,014	24,463	4,137	.28	28,314	99	198	117
13,083	21,929	4,771	.32	23,763	89	223	125
12,963	20,813	5,587	.37	20,883	79	264	136
14,259	24,426	4,674	.31	24,452	84	240	82
14,210	23,870	5,130	.34	22,910	79	263	85
12,544	20,117	5,483	.37	18,304	72	318	91
12,250	18,713	6,287	.42	16,000	64	427	99
14,308	22,736	6,464	.43	20,148	69	345	75
12,936	20,228	6,172	.41	16,896	64	427	62
12,250	18,285	6,715	.45	14,750	59	590	68

67," and Table 16, "Continued Contributions to the Individual's Retirement Account." In essence both options involve an agreement from the institution to continue contributions to an employee's annuity account until the mandatory retirement age (again assumed to be 67) if the employee retires early. If the potential early retiree accepts the arrangement, his old budget line can be used to finance the continued retirement system contribution and to hire a new employee.

Table 15 shows the option for a defined-benefit plan; Table 16, for a defined-contribution plan. In both tables the potential early retiree is receiving a 2% per year real salary increase. In Table 15, where the annuity is based on age, length of service, and highest salary, the difference between an early-retirement annuity and a mandatory-age annuity is computed. This difference is the supplemental annuity which must be purchased. The total cost, and the level annual cost, of purchasing the supplemental annuity are shown. Again, the budget line released is calculated.

In Table 16, the defined contribution example, a different approach is taken. Here it is assumed that an institution continues both the employer and the employee contribution to the retirement fund. This combined contribution is assumed to be 20% of the employee's annual salary. Thus, 80% of the budget line is released for a new hire.

These latter two options are different from the earlier options in that the early retiree receives neither an early-retirement annuity nor a pension supplement. The institution merely continues its contributions to the terminating employee's pension account, and the pension will not be paid until the mandatory retirement age. Thus, in most cases, the terminating employee would have to reemploy elsewhere.

Comparing the Alternatives

The options can be compared along several dimensions, including the funds released per early retiree, the replacements that may be hired, the early retiree's annuity income, and the institution's ability to "select" the early retirees.

Funds Released per Early Retiree. Reduction of payroll costs and the replacement of faculty members are the two primary objectives of early-retirement schemes. For each option, the payroll costs saved by the institution per person retired were calculated. In cases where an employee need not be replaced, these figures represent actual payroll savings. When an early retiree must be replaced, they represent the funds available for hiring a new faculty member.

Each alternative, for at least one age-service group, will release enough—or almost enough—money for the hiring of an assistant professor at an assumed nine-month salary of $15,000 per year. Option 1, the full-salary annuity, comes close to releasing sufficient funds for the hiring of a replacement only for persons aged 62 with thirty-two or more years of service credit. For persons aged 55 or less, the cost is greater than the funds released.

Option 2, the individual-based annuity, releases sufficient funds for persons aged 62 with between seventeen and thirty-two years of service. Almost enough funds are released for persons aged 62 with between twenty-two and twenty-seven years of service credit. No persons at age 50 or 55, no matter how many years of service credit, release enough money for hiring even a half-time replacement.

Under Option 3, the group-based annuity, the higher-paid employees tend to release more funds than lower-paid employees because of the difference in their base salaries and the greater increases given the lower-paid employees who agree to retire early. Among the lowest-paid third, there is not one age-group at which an early retiree releases sufficient funds to hire a replacement. Within the middle salary group, two cohorts release enough money to hire a replacement. And within the highest third, all but the youngest age-group release sufficient funds. Within the lowest salary group, there are several cases of a deficit, one shortfall being more than $18,000.

For Option 4, the partial employment scheme, only in the oldest age-service group does an early retirement make even a substantial contribution toward a replacement's salary. Since the current employee is rehired on a half-time basis under this alternative, the break-even point would be $7,500—enough money to hire a half-time faculty member as a replacement. This being the criterion, Option 4 is successful in four age-service groups.

Options 5 and 6, under which only continued contributions to the retiree's annuity are provided, release the most money. In every case, sufficient funds are released to hire a replacement. However, it is doubtful whether there would be enough financial incentive under these options to cause employees to terminate early.

Ability to Hire Replacements. An institution must know the percentage of persons in each age-service cohort likely to elect early retire-

Table 15 Supplemental Annuity To Continue Annuity Contributions Until Age 67

1	2	3	4	5	6	7	8	9	10	11	12
Current Age	Years Service Credit Now	Present Mean Salary for Age-Service Cohort	SLA at 67 Based on Present Salary and Service but at Age 67	Expected Salary at 67, 2%/Year Real Increase	Single Life Annuity at 67	Supplemental SLA Required at 67 (SSLA) [6−4]	Value of SSLA at 67 [7×9.384]	Present Value of SSLA at 6% Discount]	Level Annual Cost of SSLA [9÷Annuity Value]	Balance of Budget Line Released Annually [3−10]	FTE Assistant Professor at $15,000 per ER for Duration
								(.7473)	(4.4651)		
62	32	$32,500	$23,920	$35,750	$28,600	$4,680	$43,917	$32,819	$7,350	$25,150	1.68
62	27	30,400	18,878	33,440	24,612	5,734	53,808	40,211	9,006	21,394	1.43
62	22	29,500	14,927	32,450	20,152	5,225	49,031	36,641	8,206	21,294	1.42
62	17	33,500	13,099	36,850	18,646	5,547	52,053	38,899	8,712	24,788	1.65
								(.6651)	(5.9173)		
60	30	30,200	20,838	34,730	27,784	6,946	65,181	43,352	7,326	22,874	1.52
60	25	28,600	16,445	32,890	24,207	7,762	72,839	48,445	8,187	20,413	1.36
60	20	26,700	12,282	30,705	19,067	6,785	63,670	42,347	7,157	19,543	1.30
60	15	26,400	9,108	30,360	15,362	6,254	58,688	39,033	6,596	19,804	1.32
								(.4970)	(8.8869)		
55	25	29,100	16,733	36,957	29,566	12,833	120,425	59,851	6,735	22,365	1.49
55	20	29,000	13,340	36,830	27,107	13,767	129,190	64,207	7,225	21,775	1.45
55	15	25,600	8,832	32,512	20,190	11,358	106,584	52,972	5,961	19,639	1.31
55	10	25,000	5,750	31,750	16,066	10,316	96,805	48,112	5,414	19,586	1.31
								(.3713)	(11.1060)		
50	20	29,200	13,432	40,880	32,704	19,272	180,848	67,194	6,050	23,150	1.54
50	15	26,400	9,108	36,960	27,202	18,094	169,794	63,045	5,677	20,723	1.38
50	10	25,000	5,750	35,000	21,735	15,985	150,003	55,696	5,015	19,985	1.33

Note: This table is computed assuming that the supplement required will be equal to the difference between the expected annuity at age 67 and the SLA that would be received if the early retiree's account were left to accumulate until age 67. Under this option the early retiree receives no supplemental payment from the university between early retirement and the mandatory retirement age. At the mandatory retirement age, the early retiree receives the annuity he would have received had he remained employed till the mandatory retirement age and received a 2% per-year salary increase.

106

Table 16 Continued Contributions to the Individual's Retirement Account

1	2	3	4	5	6	7	8	9	10
Current Age	Years Service Credit Now	Present Mean Salary for Age-Service Cohort	Expected Salary at 67, 2%/Year Real Increase	Years till Age 67	Total Salary Now Till Age 67	Total Cost of the 20% Annuity Contribution	Present Value of the 20% Annuity Contribution	Balance of Budget Line Released Annually[a]	FTE Assistant Professor at $15,000 per ER for Duration
62	32	$32,500	$35,750	5	(5.3) $172,250	$34,450	(.8418) $29,000	$26,000	1.7
62	27	30,400	33,400	5	161,120	32,224	27,126	24,320	1.6
62	22	29,500	32,450	5	156,350	31,270	26,323	23,600	1.6
62	17	33,500	36,850	5	177,550	35,510	29,892	26,800	1.8
60	30	30,200	34,730	7	(7.58) 228,916	45,783	(.7941) 36,355	24,160	1.6
60	25	28,600	32,890	7	216,788	43,358	34,431	22,880	1.5
60	20	26,700	30,705	7	202,386	40,477	32,143	21,360	1.4
60	15	26,400	30,360	7	200,112	40,022	31,782	21,120	1.4
55	25	29,100	36,957	12	(13.68) 398,088	79,618	(.6891) 54,864	23,280	1.6
55	20	29,000	36,830	12	396,720	79,344	54,676	23,200	1.6
55	15	25,600	32,512	12	350,208	70,024	48,266	20,480	1.4
55	10	25,000	31,750	12	342,000	68,400	47,134	20,000	1.3
50	20	29,200	40,880	17	(20.41) 595,972	119,194	(.5997) 71,481	23,360	1.6
50	15	26,400	36,960	17	538,824	107,765	64,627	21,120	1.4
50	10	25,000	35,000	17	510,250	102,050	61,199	20,000	1.3

[a] Eighty percent of the early retiree's budget line is released in each case. Like the option described in Table 15, the early retiree does not receive a supplement between early retirement and the mandatory retirement age, nor does he draw an early-retirement pension.

ment in order to estimate the effectiveness of alternative plans. Since only rough estimates are available from the experiences of the few universities that have implemented these schemes, local estimates will have to be made. In making them, a university or college should recognize that the most efficient option—that is, the one with the highest replacement ratio—may encourage only a few early retirements. Option 6 frees more than enough funds per early retiree to hire a replacement employee, but relatively few persons would elect the option. On the other hand, although Option 2 releases little money per early retiree, more persons might choose it and so accelerate turnover. To use Option 2, however, an institution would have to be satisfied with less than a one-to-one replacement ratio.

In deciding which option to adopt, the needs of both the institution and the potential early retirees must be weighed. Obviously Option 1, the full-salary option, would be very attractive to employees but very expensive for the institution. The reverse would be the case for Options 5 and 6. If part-time employment is an important criterion, then Option 4 should be seriously considered. The choice between Options 2 and 3 would depend on historic salary practices at an institution (that is, do salary differences reflect merit?) and on an estimate of their appeal to current faculty members.

Early-Retirement Annuity Income. The economic incentive to retire early can be measured by the relation between the employee's annuity income from liberalized early retirement and his annuity income from normal early retirement. In only one case does the liberalized early-retirement income not exceed the normal early-retirement income. This occurs under Option 3 for the oldest and longest-term employees earning above the median salary for their age-service group. Their own normal early-retirement annuities would be greater than the incentive annuities based on the median salary for their age-service group. In practice, if these persons were to retire early, they would probably receive an annuity based on their own salary rather than on the median of their age-service cohort.

When the liberalized early-retirement income is compared with the income expected at mandatory retirement, increases are not as great. However, the incentive early annuities are close to the value of the mandatory-age annuities, and indeed this match was one of the primary factors considered in the development of the alternatives. However, the retiree receives no income under Options 5 and 6 until he reaches the mandatory retirement age.

In terms of total retirement income, Option 1, which was designed to provide an early-retirement income equal to one's preretirement income, is most attractive. However, few funds are released under this alternative. Option 4, the partial employment option, provides retirement incomes of at least two-thirds of current salary (except in the youngest age-group), but participants must work half-time to earn about 50% of this income. Option 2 provides fairly high retirement incomes, compared with present earnings, for certain age and service groups. Persons with twenty or more years of service credit receive at least two-thirds of their present salary.

In terms of retirement income as compared with present income, Option 1 would be ranked first by most persons. Option 4 would be ranked first or second by persons who would like to continue working at their university, while Option 2 would be ranked second by persons who would rather not work after early retirement. Option 3 would be ranked first by lower-paid employees but last by their higher-paid colleagues. From the early retiree's point of view, neither Option 5 nor Option 6 is likely to be very attractive. Since the retiree receives no supplement and must wait until the mandatory retirement age to draw his pension, he would certainly be reluctant to accept either of these options unless he were very close to the mandatory retirement age, had substantial savings, or planned to reemploy.

Ability to Select the Retirees. Unless an institution identifies specific employees and convinces them to accept early retirement, there is little certainty that the appropriate persons will be encouraged to take advantage of the retirement scheme. If it can be assumed that within a specific age and service cohort the more highly paid employees represent the more valued ones, then the group-based scheme may be most effective in retiring the appropriate persons. The same logic leads us to conclude that the individual-based early-retirement scheme may tend to encourage the more valued academics to retire.

The partial employment alternative falls between these extremes. Since this scheme is intended to reemploy early retirees on a part-time basis, the benefits schedule would be related to the individual rather than to the group. Thus, those who elect this option would probably be somewhat highly valued. One might argue that these are not the persons to retire on a part-time basis, that the less-valued employees should be retired partially and the highly-valued employees should be retained full-time. This need not be so, since the partial employment option could be used in conjunction with a complete retirement alternative, making it possible to retain at least some of the services of those employees who are in high demand for both campus and off-campus activities while retiring the less-valued employees. However, it is not clear that employees in high demand want to retire early.

OTHER POSSIBLE ALTERNATIVES

Other alternatives that might encourage early retirement have not been evaluated here. For example, unproductive employees might be given an annual salary *decrement* to encourage them to retire before the mandatory age. In practice, all employees might receive the same percentage decrement, and the cuts would be restored only if such action were deserved. Another option would be to require all employees to discuss their retirement plans with their superior at regular intervals. Less-productive employees might be encouraged to begin or increase payments into a supplemental retirement fund. The institution might even agree to make matching contributions if the employee agreed to retire at a certain date.

Since the financial disadvantage of early retirement can be severe if a person retires a decade or so early, partial retirement from perhaps age 55 through age 59 with complete retirement at age 60 might be desirable. Again, few persons may decide to take this route, but it may be the best course for some. Such an option might also be the only way in which to encourage some persons who now plan to continue until the mandatory age to step down early. The major difficulty with part-time reemployment seems to be determining mutually agreeable part-time tasks.

SELECTING THE OPTION

From even a strict cost standpoint, it is not easy to identify the best alternative. The choice depends on the objectives of the institution. Since these early-retirement schemes may not free sufficient funds to replace early retirees with new employees on a one-to-one basis, one of the institution's most critical tasks is to estimate the marginal productivity of both potential retirees and potential new employees. If the sum of the marginal products of the potential new employees is greater than that of the potential retirees, an early-retirement plan might be an economical means of faculty rejuvenation. The following paragraphs summarize the cost effects of the six options.

Option 1: Full-Salary Early Annuity. This alternative is undoubtedly the most favored option of potential early retirees because it makes their retirement income equal to their full salary. For the institution, it may not be a desirable alternative because it would permit only a low replacement rate.

Option 2: Individual-Based Early Annuity. This alternative saves the institution the most in salaries and allows a reasonable replacement ratio, but it may not be effective in retiring the appropriate employees. The benefits schedule gives highly-paid employees the greatest financial incentive to retire early. This scheme provides a moderate level of retirement income, and the early retiree receives these benefits with no part-time employment required.

This option illustrates, however, that it can be expensive to provide increased annuities to persons more than a few years away from the mandatory retirement age. Only for employees approximately five years from mandatory retirement are sufficient funds freed to permit the hiring of replacements on a one-to-one basis. Although this scheme may not save the institution a great deal of money, it should encourage employees to retire early. Even early retirees with relatively short periods of service receive annuities equal to two-thirds of their current salaries.

Option 3: Group-Based Early Annuity. This alternative saves the institution the least amount in salaries, but it may be able to retire the less-valued employees. This option rates below Option 2 in terms of total retirement income provided.

Option 4: Individual-Based Early Annuity with Partial Employment. This alternative ranks high in terms of savings to the institution per employee retired. To the extent that those employees who elect to participate in this alternative are more highly valued and might have retired completely if the option were not available, it is somewhat effective in retaining selected faculty members on a part-time basis. The income received by an early retiree ranges from 59% to 100% of current salary, but the early retiree must accept a part-time position to earn about half of that income.

Options 5 and 6: Continued Annuity Contributions. These options are not directly comparable with the other options because they do not provide retirement income from early retirement to mandatory retirement. The institution would be able to reallocate approximately 80% of each early retiree's salary.

Since these latter two options may appeal only to persons who have arranged for reemployment, it is conceivable that they could increase the cost of a natural process to the institution. Today, some people decide at mid-career to leave an institution and move elsewhere with no special compensation. Instead of encouraging more people to move to another institution, these options may cause the institution to compensate those persons already planning to leave. The other options, it should be recalled, have a severance payment or increased annuity intended to cause people to stop working altogether by providing them an income in lieu of salary. Some persons electing these options may already have been planning to retire early, but the added benefits are expected to encourage additional persons to step down as well. Of course, under all methods it would be necessary for the institution to establish eligibility rules and to manage the early retirements so its manpower requirements are kept in balance.

The tables presented in this chapter are only examples of how early-retirement alternatives can be compared for employees of various ages with different service and salary histories. Of course, an institution should expand these calculations to include persons with various years of service credit nearer to and further from retirement. Also, it is extremely important that these figures be computed with institution-specific data. Costs other than those of providing an increased pension should be considered: recruitment and hiring costs for replacement employees, for example. Although these costs would be incurred with mandatory retirements as well, they would be encountered earlier than planned under an early-retirement scheme.

Detailed calculations for other options and for defined-contribution plans may be found elsewhere by persons desiring to perform their own analysis.[6] The key factors to be kept in mind when replicating this analysis are:

1. Determine the level of benefits to be paid the early retiree.
2. Determine the mandatory-retirement-age pension.
3. Determine the benefits the early retiree will receive from his early-retirement pension.
4. Add social-security income to the expected benefits when appropriate.
5. Calculate the additional payment to be made to the early retiree. Determine both:

a. The additional payment made from early retirement to the mandatory retirement age.

b. The additional payment made after mandatory retirement age.

6. Determine the cost to the institution of these additional payments. The cost will vary depending on whether the payment is made in one lump sum, whether an annuity is purchased for the early retiree, whether the payment for the annuity is made in equal installments, and whether the payment is made annually from the institution's general funds. Consider:

a. The payment from early retirement to the mandatory retirement age might be paid from the early retiree's salary line, with the balance of the salary line being used to pay a replacement employee and to purchase the early retiree a supplemental pension that will go into effect at the mandatory age.

b. The early retirement payment might be paid in one year if the institution has the funds to finance the transaction. The key point will be the size of the early-retirement lump-sum payment.

If an institution is able to determine the amount of an annual supplement to be paid an employee, it can purchase such a supplement from an insurance company with a one-time payment or with level annual payments. Clearly, an institution should seek legal advice about ways to finance supplemental annuity payments.

NOTES

1. A defined-benefit annuity is one in which a member's benefits are defined by criteria such as number of years of service credit, age at retirement, and highest salary. The benefits received may exceed the actual contributions (plus earnings on contributions) to the retiree's account. A defined-contribution plan is one in which the employee's and employer's contributions (plus interest) establish the retiree's financial benefits.

2. In earlier analyses an average salary increase of 4% was assumed. This figure was probably too high for real salary increases, particularly for older faculty members. Since those earlier analyses, salary trends have been examined more closely. Although the data are sketchy, real rates (rates that do not include expected inflation) of about 3% for younger employees and of 1% to 2% for older employees might be more appropriate for near-term estimates.

3. Carl Vernon Patton, "A Seven-Day Project: Early Faculty Retirement Alternatives," *Policy Analysis* 1, no. 4 (Fall 1975): 731-753.

4. An actuarial table states the cost at various ages by sex of $1.00 of pension income paid monthly for life at a given yearly interest rate. The tables are revised periodically to reflect changing economic conditions and mortality rates.

5. Deciding which discount rate to use is troublesome because of inflation. Although the literature provides little guidance, a paper dealing with the issue has been published. It lays out an argument for using either real interest rates and real prices or nominal interest rates and nominal prices. See Steve H. Hanke, Philip H. Carver, and Paul Bugg, "Project Evaluation During Inflation," *Water Resources Research* 11, no. 4 (August 1975): 511-514.

6. For further information on the same issue see James D. Bruce, "Costs and Benefits of Early Retirement in Academia," paper presented at the 1976 Annual Meeting of the American Physical Society (New York: February 1976); Teachers Insurance and Annuity Association of America—College Retirement Equities Fund, "Bulletin: Provisions for Early Retirement" (New York: TIAA-CREF, 1972); David S. P. Hopkins, "An Early Retirement Program for the Stanford Faculty: Report and Recommendations" (Stanford, Calif.: Stanford University, Academic Planning Office, 1972); and Hans H. Jenny, *Early Retirement, a New Issue in Higher Education: The Financial Consequences of Early Retirement* (New York: TIAA—CREF, 1974).

5

Career Options and Faculty Composition

Universities and colleges became interested in ways to modify the composition of their staffs when they realized that the slowdown in higher education's expansion was beginning to reduce the number of new faculty members they could hire. Fears about the consequences of an aging faculty body were expressed, and it was commonly held that possibly even fewer new appointments would be made because the 50-to-60 age-group had more than its proportionate share of faculty members. These professors, hired *en masse* during the education boom of the 1950s and 1960s, comprised a major portion of the professorial force, the argument went, and it would be years before they would retire. Early retirement was advanced as one way to induce these persons to leave campus and increase the number of positions available for new faculty members.

This account does describe the faculty age structure and resultant problems at some colleges and universities, including some of the institutions now considering incentive early retirement. However, many institutions do not have an overrepresentation of faculty members between ages 50 and 60. When addressing the implications of an incentive early-retirement scheme both for individual institutions and all of academia, we must take into consideration the age structure of the faculty. If there are not large numbers of persons in the near-retirement years, then even highly efficient early-retirement schemes may have little effect. There simply may be too few people to attract to the alternatives. Furthermore, an induced early retirement today means one less regular retirement tomorrow.

IS THERE AN AGE PROBLEM?

Data from both an analysis of the 1972–73 American Council on Education (ACE) survey and the 1975 Carnegie Council survey of American academics indicate that university and college professors are normally distributed by age.[1] Figures 1 through 4, based on the more recent Carnegie data, summarize the age distributions for all institutions and for selected categories of institutions: High-Quality Research Universities, Medium-Quality Research Universities, and Medium-Quality Four-Year Colleges.[2] In every case, faculty members are distributed in greater percentages among the younger ages, with decreasing proportions in the older age groups, but with no substantial bulges of faculty members at any age. Any slight bulges which do exist occur at the younger ages among people not eligible for early retirement. These data suggest that the decline in the percentage of young doctorates in institutions of higher education cannot be related entirely to an overabundance of faculty members near retirement.[3]

Since these data could obscure differences among fields, we analyzed them by field within selected types of institutions. From the 1972–73 ACE data, age distributions for faculty members within the high-quality research university category were computed; age distributions by field were produced for high-quality universities, medium-quality universities and medium-quality four-year colleges using the 1975 Carnegie data. In all cases, large percentages of faculty members are not found in the age-groups near retirement. Rather, the large groupings, when they do appear, exist at the younger ages. For illustration, see the histograms by selected fields for the medium-quality universities which are presented in Figures 5 through 8.

Since these are aggregated data, differences among individual institutions may be obscured. Nonetheless, they suggest that incentive early retirement would have a limited effect on the age structure of academia, even though it might have a strong effect on the age structure at a particular institution. Differences by institution should not be overlooked, as a disproportionate share of faculty members in the older age-groups might cause staffing problems for a particular department, college, or university.

A FACULTY FLOW MODEL[4]

Colleges and universities interested in adopting incentive early-retirement programs would do well to test their probable effects with a

Figure 1
Faculty Age Distribution for All Institutions

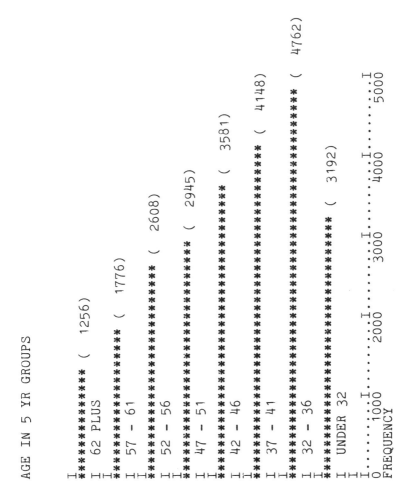

Note: Missing Observations (MO) = 730.

Source: 1975 Carnegie Council survey

Figure 2
*Faculty Age Distribution for High Quality
Research Universities*

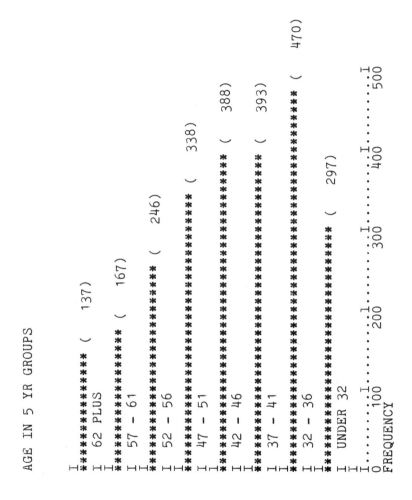

Note: MO = 76.
Source: 1975 Carnegie Council survey

Figure 3
Faculty Age Distribution for Medium Quality
Research Universities

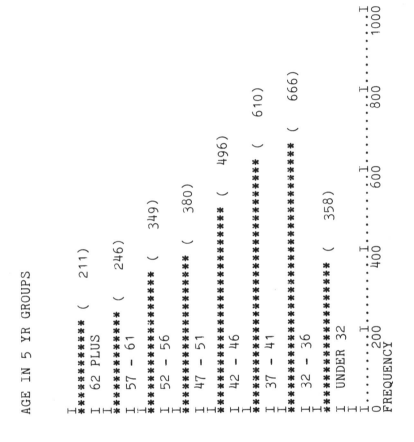

Note: MO = 81.

Source: 1975 Carnegie Council survey

Figure 4
Faculty Age Distribution for Medium Quality
Four-Year Colleges

Note: MO = 60.
Source: 1975 Carnegie Council survey

Figure 5
Faculty Age Distribution for the Biological Sciences:
Medium Quality Research Universities

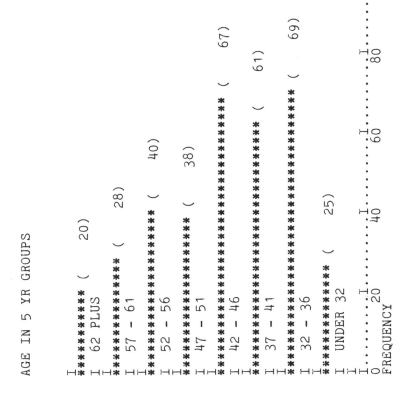

Note: MO = 9.

Source: 1975 Carnegie Council survey

As defined in the Carnegie Council survey, the Biological Sciences includes Bacteriology, Biochemistry, Biology, Botany, Physiology, Zoology, and other Biological Sciences.

Figure 6
Faculty Age Distribution for the Physical Sciences:
Medium Quality Research Universities

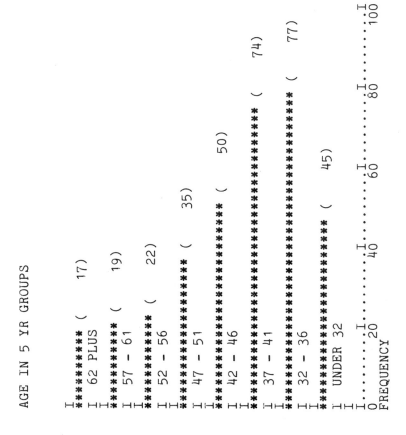

Note: MO = 5.

Source: 1975 Carnegie Council survey

As defined in the Carnegie Council survey, the Physical Sciences includes Chemistry, Geology, Physics, General Physical Science, and Mathematics/Statistics.

Figure 7
Faculty Age Distribution for the Humanities:
Medium Quality Research Universities

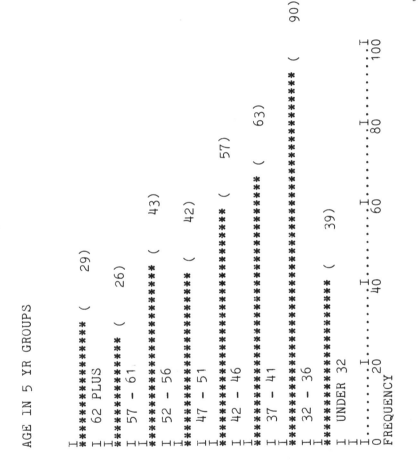

Note: MO = 8.

Source: 1975 Carnegie Council survey

As defined in the Carnegie Council survey, the Humanities includes English Language and Literature, French, German, Spanish, other foreign languages, History, Philosophy, Religion and Theology, and General Humanities.

Figure 8
Faculty Age Distribution for the Social Sciences:
Medium Quality Research Universities

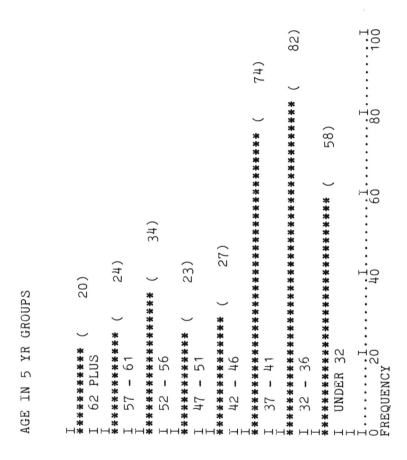

Note: MO = 4.

Source: 1975 Carnegie Council survey

As defined in the Carnegie Council survey, the Social Sciences includes Anthropology, Economics, Geography, Political Science, Psychology, Sociology, and General Social Sciences.

faculty flow model. Several models now exist.[5] Their applications have revealed a general aging trend within faculties of constant size. Unless current faculty members can be encouraged to leave the institution, the aging trend reduces the number of new hires that can be made in the near term. Older faculty members might be encouraged to retire early; younger faculty members might be denied tenure at higher rates; mid-career change programs might encourage outmigration; or other forces might cause faculty members to leave academia for other pursuits.

In these models, retirement rates have to be quite high to change the hiring rate or the age structure of the faculty. Causing faculty members to retire a few years early has limited impact, since these people would be soon leaving anyway. Furthermore, when people are induced to retire a few years early, the temporary increase in the retirement rate that results is followed by a return to the former rate as people who would have retired in years to come have already left. The greatest effect results from changing the tenure rate. If young faculty members are denied promotion and required to leave the university, high faculty turnover can be maintained—but primarily among entry-level academics.

In order to investigate the consequences of increasing the retirement rate or encouraging people to leave the university at mid-career, we produced a faculty flow model to which we could apply available aggregated data. The approach was to test the effect of alternative retirement rates, tenure-denial rates, mid-career change rates, and other factors on faculty composition. We examined the results for both a normally distributed faculty population and one with a greater proportion of older members. After testing the impact of each rate on the base populations, all other rates held constant, we investigated the interaction effect of combining rates.

Features of the Model

Factors affecting faculty growth and change were assumed to include (1) tenure decisions, (2) death and retirement, (3) outmigration (taking a position elsewhere), (4) mid-career change, and (5) new hires. The model uses a total *tenure denial rate* and a *tenure denial distribution* for the age cohorts 30 to 34 and 35 to 39. Limitations on available data forced us to restrict tenure decisions to faculty members younger than age 40. Since most tenure decisions are made before the faculty member reaches his late thirties, the model assigns more denials to the 30-to-34 cohort than to the 35-to-39 cohort.

The empirical *death and retirement rates* are the most straight-forward of all those used in our model. In the younger age cohorts, these rates exclusively represent death rates; in the older cohorts, they represent both death and retirement. These rates are applied to the population in each age cohort.

The market-induced *outmigration rate,* when applied to the total population, yields the total number of faculty members who will leave that year. This figure is then distributed throughout the entire population according to observed trends.

To illustrate the effect of mid-career change programs, we have incorporated a *mid-career change rate* into the model. This variable describes the effects of incentives to cause people between ages 40 and 50 to leave the university.

The *new hire/replacement rate* is applied to the total number of faculty members who annually leave the population. The rate is based on the percentage of all outmigrants, tenure denials, mid-career changes, and so on to be replaced with new employees (e.g., 80% to 105%). In this analysis we assume a steady-state and use 100%. These new appointments are then distributed among the age cohorts according to observed trends.

The analysis was carried out using adjusted rates from Cartter and McDowell and the Berkeley Faculty Flow Model.[6] We used a hypothetical base population from ACE data, grouped according to the Carnegie classification of High-Quality Research Universities. These age-distribution data, grouped by commonly accepted five-year intervals, were standardized to a base of 1,000 persons. The population describes a faculty where the normal retirement age is 65, the institution's mandatory retirement age is approximately 67, and the compulsory retirement age is 70. In other words, under current retirement rates, approximately two-thirds of the faculty members retire between ages 65 and 66; and that by the assumed mandatory retirement age of 67, approximately three-quarters of the faculty members have retired. Only a few persons are reappointed until age 70. The exact percentages of retirees for each age depends on the retirement rate.

Effects of Alternative Tenure Denial Rates

Experimentation with the model revealed that the total tenure-denial rate is the most sensitive variable. Figure 9 shows the input data for a projection using a normally distributed population. Figures 9a through 9d report projected distributions for three five-year intervals.

Figure 9
Faculty Age Projection: Normal Age Distribution Assuming a Low Tenure Denial Rate

BASE YEAR : 1978   NUMBER OF FIVE YEAR PROJECTIONS : 3

TOTAL TENURE DENIAL RATE : .0100

TOTAL EXPERIENCED OUTMIGRATION RATE : .0100

TOTAL REPLACEMENT RATE : 1.0000

AGE COHORT	BASE POPULATION	NEW HIRING DISTRIBUTION	OUTMIGRATION DISTRIBUTION	RETIREMENT RATES	TENURE DENIAL DISTRIBUTION	MID-CAREER RATES
70 PLUS	0.	0.0000	0.0000	1.0000	0.0000	0.0000
65 – 69	36.	0.0000	0.0000	.3374	0.0000	0.0000
60 – 64	52.	0.0000	.0100	.0653	0.0000	0.0000
55 – 59	73.	.0100	.0100	.0166	0.0000	0.0000
50 – 54	117.	.0200	.0400	.0107	0.0000	0.0000
45 – 49	132.	.0400	.0700	.0069	0.0000	0.0000
40 – 44	169.	.1000	.1500	.0044	0.0000	0.0000
35 – 39	161.	.1300	.2400	.0028	.4000	0.0000
30 – 34	166.	.3200	.2800	.0018	.6000	0.0000
UNDER 30	94.	.3800	.2000	.0016	0.0000	0.0000
TOTAL	1000.					

Figure 9a
Faculty Age Projection: Normal Distribution Assuming a Low Tenure Denial Rate

HISTORICAL BASE YEAR 1978

POPULATION TABLE

AGE COHORT	BASE POPULATION	OUTMI-GRANTS	TENURE DENIALS	RECENT RETIREES	MID-CAREER CHANGE	RECENT HIRES	NET CHANGE
70 PLUS	0.	----	----	----	----	----	----
65 - 69	36.	----	----	----	----	----	----
60 - 64	52.	----	----	----	----	----	----
55 - 59	73.	----	----	----	----	----	----
50 - 54	117.	----	----	----	----	----	----
45 - 49	132.	----	----	----	----	----	----
40 - 44	169.	----	----	----	----	----	----
35 - 39	161.	----	----	----	----	----	----
30 - 34	166.	----	----	----	----	----	----
UNDER 30	94.	----	----	----	----	----	----
TOTAL	1000.						

POPULATION HISTOGRAM

AGE COHORT	POPULATION	
70 PLUS	0.	A
65 - 69	36.	A
60 - 64	52.	AAAA
55 - 59	73.	AAAA
50 - 54	117.	AAAAA
45 - 49	132.	AAAAA
40 - 44	169.	AAAAAA
35 - 39	161.	AAAAAAAA
30 - 34	166.	AAAAAAAAAA
UNDER 30	94.	AAAAAAAAAAA
TOTAL	1000.	AAAAAAAAAAAAAAAAA

Figure 9b

Faculty Age Projection: Normal Distribution Assuming a Low Tenure Denial Rate

FIVE YEAR SUMMARY AT 1983

POPULATION TABLE

AGE COHORT	BASE POPULATION	OUTMI-GRANTS	TENURE DENIALS	RECENT RETIREES	MID-CAREER CHANGE	RECENT HIRES	NET CHANGE	RESULTING POPULATION	AGE COHORT
70 PLUS	0.	0.	0.	0.	0.	0.	0.	5.	70 PLUS
65 – 69	36.	0.	0.	31.	0.	0.	-31.	37.	65 – 69
60 – 64	52.	0.	0.	15.	0.	0.	-15.	67.	60 – 64
55 – 59	73.	0.	0.	6.	0.	1.	-5.	110.	55 – 59
50 – 54	117.	2.	0.	6.	0.	3.	-5.	127.	50 – 54
45 – 49	132.	4.	0.	5.	0.	6.	-3.	163.	45 – 49
40 – 44	169.	7.	0.	4.	0.	14.	3.	154.	40 – 44
35 – 39	161.	12.	7.	2.	0.	18.	-3.	158.	35 – 39
30 –.34	166.	14.	10.	2.	0.	44.	19.	127.	30 – 34
UNDER 30	94.	10.	0.	1.	0.	52.	41.	52.	UNDER 30
TOTAL	1000.					52.	0.	1000.	TOTAL

POPULATION HISTOGRAM

```
70 PLUS     A
            A
65 - 69     AAAA
            AAAA
60 - 64     AAAAAAA
            AAAAAAA
55 - 59     AAAAAAAAAAA
            AAAAAAAAAAA
50 - 54     AAAAAAAAAAAAA
            AAAAAAAAAAAAA
45 - 49     AAAAAAAAAAAAAAAAA
            AAAAAAAAAAAAAAAAA
40 - 44     AAAAAAAAAAAAAAAA
            AAAAAAAAAAAAAAAA
35 - 39     AAAAAAAAAAAAAAAA
            AAAAAAAAAAAAAAAA
30 - 34     AAAAAAAAAAAAA
            AAAAAAAAAAAAA
UNDER 30    AAAAA
            AAAAA
```

Figure 9c
Faculty Age Projection: Normal Distribution Assuming a Low Tenure Denial Rate

FIVE YEAR SUMMARY AT 1988

POPULATION TABLE

AGE COHORT	BASE POPULATION	OUTMI-GRANTS	TENURE DENIALS	RECENT RETIREES	MID-CAREER CHANGE	RECENT HIRES	NET CHANGE
70 PLUS	5.	0.	0.	5.	0.	0.	-5.
65 – 69	37.	0.	0.	32.	0.	0.	-32.
60 – 64	67.	0.	0.	19.	0.	0.	-20.
55 – 59	110.	0.	0.	9.	0.	2.	-8.
50 – 54	127.	2.	0.	7.	0.	3.	-6.
45 – 49	163.	4.	0.	6.	0.	6.	-3.
40 – 44	154.	7.	0.	3.	0.	15.	4.
35 – 39	158.	12.	6.	2.	0.	20.	-1.
30 – 34	127.	14.	9.	1.	0.	48.	23.
UNDER 30	52.	10.	0.	1.	0.	57.	46.
TOTAL	1000.						0.

POPULATION HISTOGRAM

```
A
A
AAAAA
AAAAA
AAAAAAAAA
AAAAAAAAAA
AAAAAAAAAAAAA
AAAAAAAAAAAAAAAAA
AAAAAAAAAAAAAAAAA
AAAAAAAAAAAAAAAA
AAAAAAAAAAAAAAAAA
AAAAAAAAAAAAA
AAAAAAAAAA
AAAAA
AAAAA
```

RESULTING POPULATION	AGE COHORT
5.	70 PLUS
47.	65 – 69
101.	60 – 64
120.	55 – 59
157.	50 – 54
149.	45 – 49
153.	40 – 44
122.	35 – 39
90.	30 – 34
57.	UNDER 30
1000.	TOTAL

130

Figure 9d
Faculty Age Projection: Normal Distribution Assuming a Low Tenure Denial Rate

FIVE YEAR SUMMARY AT 1993

POPULATION TABLE

AGE COHORT	BASE POPULATION	OUTMI-GRANTS	TENURE DENIALS	RECENT RETIREES	MID-CAREER CHANGE	RECENT HIRES	NET CHANGE	RESULTING POPULATION	AGE COHORT	POPULATION HISTOGRAM
70 PLUS	5.	0.	0.	5.	0.	0.	-5.	6.	70 PLUS	A
65 – 69	47.	0.	0.	41.	0.	0.	-41.	72.	65 – 69	AAAAAAA
60 – 64	101.	0.	0.	29.	0.	0.	-29.	109.	60 – 64	AAAAAAAAAAA
55 – 59	120.	0.	0.	10.	0.	2.	-8.	149.	55 – 59	AAAAAAAAAAAAAAA
50 – 54	157.	2.	0.	8.	0.	3.	-7.	144.	50 – 54	AAAAAAAAAAAAAA
45 – 49	149.	3.	0.	5.	0.	7.	-2.	149.	45 – 49	AAAAAAAAAAAAAAA
40 – 44	153.	7.	0.	3.	0.	17.	6.	119.	40 – 44	AAAAAAAAAAAA
35 – 39	122.	12.	6.	2.	0.	22.	3.	88.	35 – 39	AAAAAAAAA
30 – 34	90.	14.	8.	1.	0.	54.	31.	100.	30 – 34	AAAAAAAAAA
UNDER 30	57.	10.	0.	1.	0.	64.	53.	64.	UNDER 30	AAAAAA
TOTAL	1000.						0.	1000.	TOTAL	

The projection is produced by assuming a 1% annual tenure-denial rate combined with a 1% outmigration rate and a 100% replacement rate. The resulting population has a large number of faculty members in the oldest cohorts and relatively few in the younger cohorts. The bulk of the population has passed through the years of tenure decision and now represents a large group of faculty members aged 45 to 60.

We analyzed the same age distribution under different assumptions. Although we do not display the results, the model was run with a 5% tenure-denial rate with all else the same as the first projection. We found a bimodal distribution beginning to form. The upper portion centered around those aged 55 to 59 who had already been granted tenure before or during the base year. The lower portion centered around those aged 30 to 34 whose tenure decisions had not yet been made.

After analyzing projections at the 1%, 3%, 4%, 5%, 7%, and 9% levels, we decided to use a 4% annual tenure-denial rate throughout the rest of our analysis because it caused the projected population to be normally distributed and it approximated the average tenure-denial rate at several of our case institutions. (If 4% of the population at risk during a ten-year period is denied tenure each year, approximately 67% will attain tenure by the end of the risk period.)

Effects of Alternative Death and Retirement Rates

The death and retirement rates for the three oldest cohorts were varied, while the rates for the remaining cohorts were not changed. Three projections were analyzed. The first assumed rates of 5%, 10%, and 40% for the 55-to-59, 60-to-64, and 65-to-70 age cohorts, respectively; the second projection assumed 7.5%, 20%, and 60%, respectively, for the same age cohorts; and the last projection assumed 10%, 30%, and 75%, respectively.

We found that to cause a major change in the composition of the population, the death and retirement rates for the oldest three cohorts had to be changed substantially: about a 50 to 100 percent increase in the death and retirement rate for each.

Effects of Alternative Outmigration Rates

The result of an increase in the total outmigration rate was also analyzed. Populations were projected using total outmigration rates of 1% and 3%. A bimodal distribution of the population resulted from the combined effects of higher death and retirement rates coupled with the 3% outmigration rate. However, a 3% outmigration rate appears to be more than can be expected today. For this reason, the total outmigration rate was held at 1% throughout the rest of the analysis. (In most institutions, the present rate probably does not exceed 1.5%.) Rather than assuming a large increase in this rate (which applies to all age groups), one could instead effect outmigration by encouraging mid-career change for people at those ages at which outmigration would be worth the effort and money spent inducing them to leave.

Effects of Alternative Mid-Career Change Rates

Mid-career change rates eventually affect the older ages of the population distribution as well as have an immediate effect on younger faculty members. The number of older faculty members will eventually decrease, while the number of younger faculty members will increase as a result of the greater proportion of new appointments made in the younger age-groups. Projections were conducted using 1%, 2%, and 3% respectively as mid-career change rates. For all further analysis, we used mid-career change rates of 2%. This projection yielded a normal population distribution, and it is hard to believe that a higher rate could be induced, no matter how much money a university or college might spend.

Effects of Alternative Rates on an Older Population

After analyzing rates applied to a normally distributed faculty population, we analyzed how they affected an older distribution. A faculty with a normal retirement age of 65 was used, but its median age was approximately five years above that of the normally distributed faculty population. We used the distribution of one of our case institutions standardized to a population of 1,000 persons.

Alternative projections of this older distribution were made using 1%, 2%, and 3% mid-career change rates. The projections describe a faculty beginning to grow younger as the result of mid-career change. Since professors must pass through the mid-career change "filter," fewer of them move into the older age cohorts. This reduction yields vacancies which are filled primarily by younger persons. By applying certain rates, the older population distribution can be made to gradually grow younger and to finally become normally distributed. For example, Figures 10 through 10d show the effect of increased retirement rates and 2% mid-career change on an older faculty.

Figure 10
Faculty Age Projection: Older Distribution Assuming High Death and Retirement Rates

BASE YEAR : 1978   NUMBER OF FIVE YEAR PROJECTIONS : 3

TOTAL TENURE DENIAL RATE : .0400

TOTAL EXPERIENCED OUTMIGRATION RATE : .0100

TOTAL REPLACEMENT RATE : 1.0000

AGE COHORT	BASE POPULATION	NEW HIRING DISTRIBUTION	OUTMIGRATION DISTRIBUTION	RETIREMENT RATES	TENURE DENIAL DISTRIBUTION	MID-CAREER RATES
70 PLUS	0.	0.0000	0.0000	1.0000	0.0000	0.0000
65 - 69	0.	0.0000	0.0000	.6700	0.0000	0.0000
60 - 64	30.	0.0000	.0100	.2000	0.0000	0.0000
55 - 59	110.	.0100	.0100	.1000	0.0000	0.0000
50 - 54	200.	.0200	.0400	.0107	0.0000	0.0000
45 - 49	190.	.0400	.0700	.0069	0.0000	.0200
40 - 44	160.	.1000	.1500	.0044	0.0000	.0200
35 - 39	150.	.1300	.2400	.0028	.4000	0.0000
30 - 34	110.	.3200	.2800	.0018	.6000	0.0000
UNDER 30	50.	.3800	.2000	.0016	0.0000	0.0000
TOTAL	1000.					

Figure 10a
Faculty Age Projection: Older Distribution Assuming High Death and Retirement Rates

HISTORICAL BASE YEAR 1978

POPULATION TABLE

AGE COHORT	BASE POPULATION	OUTMI-GRANTS	TENURE DENIALS	RECENT RETIRES	MID-CAREER CHANGE	RECENT HIRES	NET CHANGE
70 PLUS	0.	----	----	----	----	----	----
65 - 69	0.	----	----	----	----	----	----
60 - 64	30.	----	----	----	----	----	----
55 - 59	110.	----	----	----	----	----	----
50 - 54	200.	----	----	----	----	----	----
45 - 49	190.	----	----	----	----	----	----
40 - 44	160.	----	----	----	----	----	----
35 - 39	150.	----	----	----	----	----	----
30 - 34	110.	----	----	----	----	----	----
UNDER 30	50.	----	----	----	----	----	----
TOTAL	1000.						

POPULATION HISTOGRAM

AGE COHORT	POPULATION	
70 PLUS	0.	A
65 - 69	0.	A
60 - 64	30.	AAA
55 - 59	110.	AAAAAAAAAA
50 - 54	200.	AAAAAAAAAAAAAAAAAAAA
45 - 49	190.	AAAAAAAAAAAAAAAAAAA
40 - 44	160.	AAAAAAAAAAAAAAAA
35 - 39	150.	AAAAAAAAAAAAAAA
30 - 34	110.	AAAAAAAAAAA
UNDER 30	50.	AAAAA
TOTAL	1000.	

135

Figure 10b
Faculty Age Projection: Older Distribution Assuming High Death and Retirement Rates

FIVE YEAR SUMMARY AT 1983

POPULATION TABLE

AGE COHORT	BASE POPULATION	OUTMI-GRANTS	TENURE DENIALS	RECENT RETIREES	MID-CAREER CHANGE	RECENT HIRES	NET CHANGE
70 PLUS	0.	0.	0.	0.	0.	0.	0.
65 – 69	0.	0.	0.	0.	0.	0.	0.
60 – 64	30.	0.	0.	20.	0.	0.	-21.
55 – 59	110.	0.	0.	45.	0.	2.	-44.
50 – 54	200.	2.	0.	11.	0.	5.	-8.
45 – 49	190.	4.	0.	6.	18.	9.	-19.
40 – 44	160.	7.	0.	3.	16.	23.	-3.
35 – 39	150.	12.	24.	2.	0.	31.	-8.
30 – 34	110.	14.	37.	1.	0.	75.	23.
UNDER 30	50.	10.	0.	1.	0.	89.	79.
TOTAL	1000.						0.

POPULATION HISTOGRAM

RESULTING POPULATION		AGE COHORT
0.	A	70 PLUS
9.	A	65 – 69
64.	AAAAAA	60 – 64
190.	AAAAAAAAAAAAAAAAAAAAAA	55 – 59
167.	AAAAAAAAAAAAAAAAAAAA	50 – 54
142.	AAAAAAAAAAAAAAAAA	45 – 49
135.	AAAAAAAAAAAAAAAA	40 – 44
89.	AAAAAAAAAA	35 – 39
115.	AAAAAAAAAAAAAA	30 – 34
89.	AAAAAAAAAA	UNDER 30
1000.		TOTAL

136

Figure 10c
Faculty Age Projection: Older Distribution Assuming High Death and Retirement Rates

FIVE YEAR SUMMARY AT 1988

POPULATION TABLE

AGE COHORT	BASE POPULATION	OUTMI-GRANTS	TENURE DENIALS	RECENT RETIREES	MID-CAREER CHANGE	RECENT HIRES	NET CHANGE	RESULTING POPULATION	AGE COHORT
70 PLUS	0.	0.	0.	0.	0.	0.	0.	0.	70 PLUS
65 – 69	9.	0.	0.	9.	0.	0.	-9.	21.	65 – 69
60 – 64	64.	0.	0.	43.	0.	0.	-43.	111.	60 – 64
55 – 59	190.	0.	0.	78.	0.	3.	-76.	159.	55 – 59
50 – 54	167.	2.	0.	9.	0.	5.	-5.	126.	50 – 54
45 – 49	142.	4.	0.	5.	14.	11.	-11.	122.	45 – 49
40 – 44	135.	7.	0.	3.	14.	27.	3.	85.	40 – 44
35 – 39	89.	12.	18.	1.	0.	36.	4.	107.	35 – 39
30 – 34	115.	14.	27.	1.	0.	88.	45.	166.	30 – 34
UNDER 30	89.	10.	0.	1.	0.	104.	93.	104.	UNDER 30
TOTAL	1000.						0.	1000.	TOTAL

POPULATION HISTOGRAM

```
70 PLUS    A
65 – 69    A
           A
60 – 64    AA
           AA
55 – 59    AAAAAAAAA
           AAAAAAAAAA
50 – 54    AAAAAAAAAAAAAAAAAAA
           AAAAAAAAAAAAAAAAAA
45 – 49    AAAAAAAAAAAAAAAA
           AAAAAAAAAAAAAA
40 – 44    AAAAAAAA
           AAAAAAAA
35 – 39    AAAAAAAAAAAAAAA
           AAAAAAAAAAAAAAAAA
30 – 34    AAAAAAAAAAAAAAAAAAAAAAAA
           AAAAAAAAAAAAAAAAAAAAAAAAA
UNDER 30   AAAAAAAAAA
           AAAAAAAAAA
```

137

Figure 10d
Faculty Age Projection: Older Distribution Assuming High Death and Retirement Rates

FIVE YEAR SUMMARY AT 1993

POPULATION TABLE

AGE COHORT	BASE POPULATION	OUTMI-GRANTS	TENURE DENIALS	RECENT RETIREES	MID-CAREER CHANGE	RECENT HIRES	NET CHANGE	POPULATION HISTOGRAM	RESULTING POPULATION	AGE COHORT
70 PLUS	0.	0.	0.	0.	0.	0.	0.	A	0.	70 PLUS
65 – 69	21.	0.	0.	21.	0.	0.	-21.	A	36.	65 – 69
60 – 64	111.	0.	0.	75.	0.	0.	-75.	AAAA	93.	60 – 64
55 – 59	159.	0.	0.	65.	0.	3.	-63.	AAAAAAAA	120.	55 – 59
50 – 54	126.	2.	0.	7.	0.	6.	-3.	AAAAAAAAAAA	108.	50 – 54
45 – 49	122.	3.	0.	4.	12.	12.	-8.	AAAAAAAA	78.	45 – 49
40 – 44	85.	7.	0.	2.	9.	29.	10.	AAAAAAAAAAA	107.	40 – 44
35 – 39	107.	12.	16.	2.	0.	38.	8.	AAAAAAAAAAAAAAAA	163.	35 – 39
30 – 34	166.	14.	24.	2.	0.	93.	53.	AAAAAAAAAAAAAAAAAAA	186.	30 – 34
UNDER 30	104.	10.	0.	1.	0.	110.	99.	AAAAAAAAAAA	110.	UNDER 30
TOTAL	1000.						0.		1000.	TOTAL

138

Testing the Impact of the "Proper" Rates

The changes in faculty composition which would be brought about by a mid-career change program and incentive early retirement are illustrated in Figures 11 through 11d for a normally distributed faculty. Death and retirement rates of 10%, 20%, and 67% arc assumed for the three oldest age categories. The mid-career change rate is set at 2% for both the 40-to-44 and 45-to-49 age-groups. Current outmigration, tenure-denial, and new appointment distributions are assumed.

Compared with projections assuming no increase in the retirement rate and no mid-career change, these projections show an increase in the number of near-term appointments that can be made. For example, compared to the projection described in Figures 12 through 12e, these higher rates cause the number of new appointments made during the first five years to increase by 43%. During the second five-year period this increase is 29%, and during the third it is 26%. These figures show the dampening effect mentioned earlier: boosting the retirement rate causes an initial increase in the number of appointments that can be made, but eventually the effect wears off as the population distribution grows younger and fewer persons are available for retirement. Nonetheless, induced early retirement and mid-career change can increase the near-term appointment rate.

These rates should not be sought at every institution. They merely describe the changes that can be brought about through various policies. The desired faculty structure varies from institution to institution, and so do the desired retirement and mid-career change rates. Remember also that the analysis presented here assumes a 100% replacement rate. If retirees are not replaced on a one-to-one basis, the increased turnover caused by inducing early retirements can be lost. Because of space limitations, such consequences are not modeled here.

RAISING THE MANDATORY RETIREMENT AGE

Although many institutions and faculty members are interested in finding ways to enable earlier retirement, other persons are pressing for an abolition of, or at least a further increase in the mandatory retirement age. What will happen to the age distribution of American academics after the mandatory retirement age is increased in 1982? If the change causes a large proportion of faculty members to stay on until the mandatory retirement age, one obvious result will be a decrease in the

Figure 11
Faculty Age Projection: Normal Distribution Assuming High Death and Retirement Rates

BASE YEAR : 1978   NUMBER OF FIVE YEAR PROJECTIONS : 3

TOTAL TENURE DENIAL RATE :   .0400

TOTAL EXPERIENCED OUTMIGRATION RATE :   .0100

TOTAL REPLACEMENT RATE : 1.0000

AGE COHORT	BASE POPULATION	NEW HIRING DISTRIBUTION	OUTMIGRATION DISTRIBUTION	RETIREMENT RATES	TENURE DENIAL DISTRIBUTION	MID-CAREER RATES
70 PLUS	0.	0.0000	0.0000	1.0000	0.0000	0.0000
65 – 69	36.	0.0000	0.0000	.6700	0.0000	0.0000
60 – 64	52.	0.0000	.0100	.2000	0.0000	0.0000
55 – 59	73.	.0100	.0100	.1000	0.0000	0.0000
50 – 54	117.	.0200	.0400	.0107	0.0000	0.0000
45 – 49	132.	.0400	.0700	.0069	0.0000	.0200
40 – 44	169.	.1000	.1500	.0044	0.0000	.0200
35 – 39	161.	.1300	.2400	.0028	.4000	0.0000
30 – 34	166.	.3200	.2800	.0018	.6000	0.0000
UNDER 30	94.	.3800	.2000	.0016	0.0000	0.0000
TOTAL	1000.					

Figure 11a

Faculty Age Projection: Normal Distribution Assuming High Death and Retirement Rates

HISTORICAL BASE YEAR 1978

POPULATION TABLE

AGE COHORT	BASE POPULATION	OUTMI-GRANTS	TENURE DENIALS	RECENT RETIREES	MID-CAREER CHANGE	RECENT HIRES	NET CHANGE
70 PLUS	0.	----	----	----	----	----	----
65 - 69	36.	----	----	----	----	----	----
60 - 64	52.	----	----	----	----	----	----
55 - 59	73.	----	----	----	----	----	----
50 - 54	117.	----	----	----	----	----	----
45 - 49	132.	----	----	----	----	----	----
40 - 44	169.	----	----	----	----	----	----
35 - 39	161.	----	----	----	----	----	----
30 - 34	166.	----	----	----	----	----	----
UNDER 30	94.	----	----	----	----	----	----
TOTAL	1000.						----

POPULATION HISTOGRAM

AGE COHORT	POPULATION	HISTOGRAM
70 PLUS	0.	A
65 - 69	36.	AAAA
60 - 64	52.	AAAAAA
55 - 59	73.	AAAAAAAA
50 - 54	117.	AAAAAAAAAAAAAA
45 - 49	132.	AAAAAAAAAAAAAAAA
40 - 44	169.	AAAAAAAAAAAAAAAAAAAA
35 - 39	161.	AAAAAAAAAAAAAAAAAAA
30 - 34	166.	AAAAAAAAAAAAAAAAAAAA
UNDER 30	94.	AAAAAAAAAAA
TOTAL	1000.	

Figure 1b
Faculty Age Projection: Normal Distribution Assuming High Death and Retirement Rates

POPULATION TABLE

FIVE YEAR SUMMARY AT 1983

POPULATION HISTOGRAM

AGE COHORT	BASE POPULATION	OUTMI-GRANTS	TENURE DENIALS	RECENT RETIREES	MID-CAREER CHANGE	RECENT HIRES	NET CHANGE	RESULTING POPULATION	POPULATION HISTOGRAM	AGE COHORT
70 PLUS	0.	0.	0.	0.	0.	0.	0.	0.	A	70 PLUS
65 – 69	36.	0.	0.	36.	0.	0.	-36.	17.	AA	65 – 69
60 – 64	52.	0.	0.	35.	0.	0.	-35.	42.	AAAA	60 – 64
55 – 59	73.	0.	0.	30.	0.	3.	-28.	111.	AAAAAAAAAAA	55 – 59
50 – 54	117.	2.	0.	6.	0.	5.	-3.	117.	AAAAAAAAAAAA	50 – 54
45 – 49	132.	4.	0.	4.	13.	11.	-10.	151.	AAAAAAAAAAAAAAA	45 – 49
40 – 44	169.	7.	0.	4.	17.	27.	-2.	147.	AAAAAAAAAAAAAAA	40 – 44
35 – 39	161.	12.	26.	2.	0.	35.	-6.	145.	AAAAAAAAAAAAAAA	35 – 39
30 – 34	166.	14.	40.	2.	0.	85.	30.	168.	AAAAAAAAAAAAAAAAA	30 – 34
UNDER 30	94.	10.	0.	1.	0.	101.	90.	101.	AAAAAAAAAA	UNDER 30
TOTAL	1000.						0.	1000.		TOTAL

Figure 11c
Faculty Age Projection: Normal Distribution Assuming High Death and Retirement Rates

FIVE YEAR SUMMARY AT 1988

POPULATION TABLE

AGE COHORT	BASE POPULATION	OUTMI-GRANTS	TENURE DENIALS	RECENT RETIREES	MID-CAREER CHANGE	RECENT HIRES	NET CHANGE
70 PLUS	0.	0.	0.	0.	0.	0.	0.
65 - 69	17.	0.	0.	17.	0.	0.	-17.
60 - 64	42.	0.	0.	28.	0.	0.	-29.
55 - 59	111.	0.	0.	46.	0.	2.	-44.
50 - 54	117.	2.	0.	6.	0.	5.	-3.
45 - 49	151.	4.	0.	5.	15.	10.	-13.
40 - 44	147.	7.	0.	3.	15.	25.	-1.
35 - 39	145.	12.	23.	2.	0.	32.	-5.
30 - 34	168.	14.	35.	2.	0.	79.	29.
UNDER 30	101.	10.	0.	1.	0.	94.	83.
TOTAL	1000.						0.

POPULATION HISTOGRAM

RESULTING POPULATION	AGE COHORT	HISTOGRAM
0.	70 PLUS	A
13.	65 - 69	A
65.	60 - 64	AAAAAA
111.	55 - 59	AAAAAAAAAAA
133.	50 - 54	AAAAAAAAAAAAA
131.	45 - 49	AAAAAAAAAAAAA
133.	40 - 44	AAAAAAAAAAAAA
150.	35 - 39	AAAAAAAAAAAAAAA
169.	30 - 34	AAAAAAAAAAAAAAAAA
94.	UNDER 30	AAAAAAAAA
1000.	TOTAL	

143

Figure 11d
Faculty Age Projection: Normal Distribution Assuming High Death and Retirement Rates

FIVE YEAR SUMMARY AT 1993

POPULATION TABLE

AGE COHORT	BASE POPULATION	OUTMI- GRANTS	TENURE DENIALS	RECENT RETIREES	MID-CAREER CHANGE	RECENT HIRES	NET CHANGE
70 PLUS	0.	0.	0.	0.	0.	0.	0.
65 – 69	13.	0.	0.	13.	0.	0.	-13.
60 – 64	65.	0.	0.	43.	0.	0.	-44.
55 – 59	111.	0.	0.	46.	0.	3.	-44.
50 – 54	133.	2.	0.	7.	0.	5.	-4.
45 – 49	131.	3.	0.	4.	13.	10.	-10.
40 – 44	133.	7.	0.	3.	13.	25.	2.
35 – 39	150.	12.	23.	2.	0.	33.	-4.
30 – 34	169.	14.	34.	2.	0.	82.	32.
UNDER 30	94.	10.	0.	1.	0.	97.	86.
TOTAL	1000.						0.

POPULATION HISTOGRAM

RESULTING POPULATION	AGE COHORT	POPULATION HISTOGRAM
0.	70 PLUS	A
21.	65 – 69	A AA
65.	60 – 64	AA AAAAAA AAAAAA
127.	55 – 59	AAAAAAAAAAAAAA
116.	50 – 54	AAAAAAAAAAAA AAAAAAAAAAAA
119.	45 – 49	AAAAAAAAAAAA AAAAAAAAAAAAAA
138.	40 – 44	AAAAAAAAAAAAAAA AAAAAAAAAAAAAAA
153.	35 – 39	AAAAAAAAAAAAAAAAAA AAAAAAAAAAAAAAAAAA
165.	30 – 34	AAAAAAAAAAAAAAAAAAAA AAAAAAAAAA
97.	UNDER 30	AAAAAAAAAA AAAAAAAAAA
1000.	TOTAL	

144

number of new faculty members who can be hired. But the consequences of an increase in the mandatory retirement age cannot be easily predicted because of the difficulty of estimating when persons will retire.

The increase in the mandatory retirement age may have several outcomes. Faculty members might decide to immediately extend their retirement dates. On the other hand, most might retire as now planned. The most likely reaction might be a gradual shift in the norm for academic retirement. After the age is raised, some people will undoubtedly postpone their retirements. Others, having made plans to retire at age 65 or earlier, might continue with their plans. The younger employees, with many years to plan for retirement, might adopt age 70 as a new norm.

To investigate this issue, the model was run with the normal retirement age increased to age 70. We illustrate the extreme case, in which academics take the option to work five years beyond their current planned retirement age. However, we assume that persons planning to retire before age 60 would not be affected by a change in the Age Discrimination in Employment Act.

Like the other rates we tested in this chapter, these were meant to illustrate possible results, not to predict what would actually happen. Figures 12 and 13 through 12e and 13e compare normal retirement at ages 65 and 70. Using the normally distributed base population, both projections assume a 4% tenure-denial rate, a 1% outmigration rate, no mid-career change, and 100% replacement. The projection with retirement at age 65 assumes current retirement rates. The projection with retirement at age 70 assumes persons planning to retire at age 60 or older would postpone their retirement by five years. Consequences are shown for the fifth, tenth, twentieth, thirtieth, and fortieth years. Of course, such long range projections based on an assumption of current rates will be in error. The point, though, is to illustrate the relative effect of an increase in the normal retirement age as a result of increasing or abolishing the mandatory retirement age.

In comparing the population distributions for the projected years (both projections began with the same population distribution as used in Figures 9a and 11a), one observes an initial impact of age-70 mandatory retirement and an eventual dampening. The number of new appointments that can be made annually is reduced in the near term. But eventually the persons who postponed their retirements retire, and there is a convergence between the retirement rates in the age 65 and age 70 models. For example, during the first five-year period the number of new appointments is reduced by 18%. During the next two five-year periods

Figure 12
Faculty Age Projection: Normal Distribution Assuming Normal Retirement at Age 65

BASE YEAR : 1978   NUMBER OF FIVE YEAR PROJECTIONS : 8

TOTAL TENURE DENIAL RATE : .0400

TOTAL EXPERIENCED OUTMIGRATION RATE : .0100

TOTAL REPLACEMENT RATE : 1.0000

AGE COHORT	BASE POPULATION	NEW HIRING DISTRIBUTION	OUTMIGRATION DISTRIBUTION	RETIREMENT RATES	TENURE DENIAL DISTRIBUTION	MID-CAREER RATES
70 PLUS	0.	0.0000	0.0000	1.0000	0.0000	0.0000
65 – 69	36.	0.0000	0.0000	.3374	0.0000	0.0000
60 – 64	52.	0.0000	.0100	.0653	0.0000	0.0000
55 – 59	73.	.0100	.0100	.0166	0.0000	0.0000
50 – 54	117.	.0200	.0400	.0107	0.0000	0.0000
45 – 49	132.	.0400	.0700	.0069	0.0000	0.0000
40 – 44	169.	.1000	.1500	.0044	0.0000	0.0000
35 – 39	161.	.1300	.2400	.0028	.4000	0.0000
30 – 34	166.	.3200	.2800	.0018	.6000	0.0000
UNDER 30	94.	.3800	.2000	.0016	0.0000	0.0000
TOTAL	1000.					

Figure 13
Faculty Age Projection: Normal Distribution Assuming Normal Retirement at Age 70

BASE YEAR : 1978   NUMBER OF FIVE YEAR PROJECTIONS : 8

TOTAL TENURE DENIAL RATE : .0400

TOTAL EXPERIENCED OUTMIGRATION RATE : .0100

TOTAL REPLACEMENT RATE : 1.0000

AGE COHORT	BASE POPULATION	NEW HIRING DISTRIBUTION	OUTMIGRATION DISTRIBUTION	RETIREMENT RATES	TENURE DENIAL DISTRIBUTION	MID-CAREER RATES
70 PLUS	0.	0.0000	0.0000	.3374	0.0000	0.0000
65 – 69	36.	0.0000	0.0000	.0653	0.0000	0.0000
60 – 64	52.	0.0000	.0100	.0166	0.0000	0.0000
55 – 59	73.	.0100	.0100	.0166	0.0000	0.0000
50 – 54	117.	.0200	.0400	.0107	0.0000	0.0000
45 – 49	132.	.0400	.0700	.0069	0.0000	0.0000
40 – 44	169.	.1000	.1500	.0044	0.0000	0.0000
35 – 39	161.	.1300	.2400	.0028	.4000	0.0000
30 – 34	166.	.3200	.2800	.0018	.6000	0.0000
UNDER 30	94.	.3800	.2000	.0016	0.0000	0.0000
TOTAL	1000.					

Figure 12a
Faculty Age Projection: Normal Distribution Assuming Normal Retirement at Age 65

FIVE YEAR SUMMARY AT 1983

POPULATION TABLE

AGE COHORT	BASE POPULATION	OUTMI-GRANTS	TENURE DENIALS	RECENT RETIREES	MID-CAREER CHANGE	RECENT HIRES	NET CHANGE		RESULTING POPULATION	AGE COHORT
70 PLUS	0.	0.	0.	0.	0.	0.	0.		5.	70 PLUS
65 – 69	36.	0.	0.	31.	0.	0.	-31.		37.	65 – 69
60 – 64	52.	0.	0.	15.	0.	0.	-15.		67.	60 – 64
55 – 59	73.	0.	0.	6.	0.	2.	-5.		111.	55 – 59
50 – 54	117.	2.	0.	6.	0.	4.	-4.		128.	50 – 54
45 – 49	132.	4.	0.	5.	0.	7.	-1.		165.	45 – 49
40 – 44	169.	7.	0.	4.	0.	19.	7.		139.	40 – 44
35 – 39	161.	12.	26.	2.	0.	24.	-16.		135.	35 – 39
30 – 34	166.	14.	39.	2.	0.	60.	5.		143.	30 – 34
UNDER 30	94.	10.	0.	1.	0.	60.	60.		71.	UNDER 30
TOTAL	1000.					71.	0.		1000.	TOTAL

POPULATION HISTOGRAM

```
70 PLUS    A
65 – 69    A
60 – 64    AAAA
55 – 59    AAAA
50 – 54    AAAAAAA
45 – 49    AAAAAAA
40 – 44    AAAAAAAAAAA
35 – 39    AAAAAAAAAAAAA
30 – 34    AAAAAAAAAAAAAAA
UNDER 30   AAAAAAAAAAAAAAAAA
           AAAAAAAAAAAAAAAAAAA
           AAAAAAAAAAAAAAAAAAAAA
           AAAAAAAAAAAAAAAAA
           AAAAAAAAAAAAAAA
           AAAAAAAAAAAAAAA
           AAAAAAAAAAAAA
           AAAAAAA
           AAAAAA
```

148

Figure 13a
Faculty Age Projection: Normal Distribution Assuming Normal Retirement at Age 70

FIVE YEAR SUMMARY AT 1983

POPULATION TABLE

AGE COHORT	BASE POPULATION	OUTMI-GRANTS	TENURE DENIALS	RECENT RETIREES	MID-CAREER CHANGE	RECENT HIRES	NET CHANGE	RESULTING POPULATION	AGE COHORT
70 PLUS	0.	0.	0.	0.	0.	0.	0.	26.	70 PLUS
65 – 69	36.	0.	0.	10.	0.	0.	-10.	47.	65 – 69
60 – 64	52.	0.	0.	4.	0.	0.	-5.	67.	60 – 64
55 – 59	73.	0.	0.	6.	0.	2.	-5.	110.	55 – 59
50 – 54	117.	2.	0.	6.	0.	3.	-5.	127.	50 – 54
45 – 49	132.	4.	0.	5.	0.	6.	-2.	164.	45 – 49
40 – 44	169.	7.	0.	4.	0.	15.	4.	136.	40 – 44
35 – 39	161.	12.	26.	2.	0.	20.	-20.	132.	35 – 39
30 – 34	166.	14.	39.	1.	0.	49.	-5.	132.	30 – 34
UNDER 30	94.	10.	0.	1.	0.	59.	48.	59.	UNDER 30
TOTAL	1000.						0.	1000.	TOTAL

POPULATION HISTOGRAM

```
70 PLUS    AAA
65 – 69    AAAAA
60 – 64    AAAAAAA
55 – 59    AAAAAAAAAAA
50 – 54    AAAAAAAAAAAAA
45 – 49    AAAAAAAAAAAAAAAAA
40 – 44    AAAAAAAAAAAAAA
35 – 39    AAAAAAAAAAAAA
30 – 34    AAAAAAAAAAAAA
UNDER 30   AAAAAA
```

Figure 12b
Faculty Age Projection: Normal Distribution Assuming Normal Retirement at Age 65

FIVE YEAR SUMMARY AT 1988

POPULATION TABLE

AGE COHORT	BASE POPULATION	OUTMI-GRANTS	TENURE DENIALS	RECENT RETIREES	MID-CAREER CHANGE	RECENT HIRES	NET CHANGE	RESULTING POPULATION	AGE COHORT	POPULATION HISTOGRAM
70 PLUS	5.	0.	0.	5.	0.	0.	-5.	5.	70 PLUS	A
65 – 69	37.	0.	0.	32.	0.	0.	-32.	47.	65 – 69	AAAAA
60 – 64	67.	0.	0.	19.	0.	0.	-20.	101.	60 – 64	AAAAAAAAAA
55 – 59	111.	0.	0.	9.	0.	2.	-8.	121.	55 – 59	AAAAAAAAAAAA
50 – 54	128.	2.	0.	7.	0.	4.	-5.	160.	50 – 54	AAAAAAAAAAAAAAAA
45 – 49	165.	4.	0.	6.	0.	8.	-2.	136.	45 – 49	AAAAAAAAAAAAAA
40 – 44	139.	7.	0.	3.	0.	19.	8.	118.	40 – 44	AAAAAAAAAAAA
35 – 39	135.	12.	22.	2.	0.	25.	-11.	119.	35 – 39	AAAAAAAAAAAA
30 – 34	143.	14.	33.	1.	0.	61.	12.	121.	30 – 34	AAAAAAAAAAAA
UNDER 30	71.	10.	0.	1.	0.	72.	61.	72.	UNDER 30	AAAAAAA
TOTAL	1000.						0.	1000.	TOTAL	

150

Figure 13b
Faculty Age Projection: Normal Distribution Assuming Normal Retirement at Age 70

FIVE YEAR SUMMARY AT 1988

POPULATION TABLE

AGE COHORT	BASE POPULATION	OUTMI- GRANTS	TENURE DENIALS	RECENT RETIREES	MID-CAREER CHANGE	RECENT HIRES	NET CHANGE	RESULTING POPULATION	AGE COHORT
70 PLUS	26.	0.	0.	22.	0.	0.	-22.	37.	70 PLUS
65 – 69	47.	0.	0.	14.	0.	0.	-14.	61.	65 – 69
60 – 64	67.	0.	0.	5.	0.	0.	-6.	101.	60 – 64
55 – 59	110.	0.	0.	9.	0.	2.	-8.	120.	55 – 59
50 – 54	127.	2.	0.	7.	0.	3.	-5.	158.	50 – 54
45 – 49	164.	4.	0.	6.	0.	7.	-2.	133.	45 – 49
40 – 44	136.	7.	0.	3.	0.	17.	7.	114.	40 – 44
35 – 39	132.	12.	21.	2.	0.	22.	-13.	108.	35 – 39
30 – 34	132.	14.	32.	1.	0.	55.	8.	103.	30 – 34
UNDER 30	59.	10.	0.	1.	0.	66.	55.	66.	UNDER 30
TOTAL	1000.					66.	0.	1000.	TOTAL

POPULATION HISTOGRAM

```
AAAA
AAAA
AAAAAA
AAAAAAAAAA
AAAAAAAAAA
AAAAAAAAAAAAAAAAAAAA
AAAAAAAAAAAAAAAAAAAA
AAAAAAAAAAAAAAAA
AAAAAAAAAAAAAA
AAAAAAAAAAAAAA
AAAAAAAA
AAAAAAA
```

Figure 12c
Faculty Age Projection: Normal Distribution Assuming Normal Retirement at Age 65

FIVE YEAR SUMMARY AT 1998

POPULATION TABLE

AGE COHORT	BASE POPULATION	OUTMI-GRANTS	TENURE DENIALS	RECENT RETIREES	MID-CAREER CHANGE	RECENT HIRES	NET CHANGE	POPULATION HISTOGRAM	RESULTING POPULATION	AGE COHORT
70 PLUS	6.	0.	0.	6.	0.	0.	-6.	A	9.	70 PLUS
65 – 69	72.	0.	0.	63.	0.	0.	-63.	A AAAAAAAA	78.	65 – 69
60 – 64	111.	0.	0.	32.	0.	0.	-32.	AAAAAAAAAAAAAAAAAA	139.	60 – 64
55 – 59	151.	0.	0.	12.	0.	2.	-10.	AAAAAAAAAAAAAAAA	125.	55 – 59
50 – 54	132.	2.	0.	7.	0.	4.	-5.	AAAAAAAAAAAAAAA	113.	50 – 54
45 – 49	116.	3.	0.	4.	0.	9.	1.	AAAAAAAAAAAAAA	105.	45 – 49
40 – 44	106.	7.	0.	2.	0.	22.	12.	AAAAAAAAAAAA	94.	40 – 44
35 – 39	103.	12.	17.	1.	0.	29.	-2.	AAAAAAAAAAAAAAA	113.	35 – 39
30 – 34	126.	14.	26.	1.	0.	71.	30.	AAAAAAAAAAAAAAAAAA	137.	30 – 34
UNDER 30	77.	10.	0.	1.	0.	85.	74.	AAAAAAAAAAA	85.	UNDER 30
TOTAL	1000.						0.		1000.	TOTAL

Figure 13c
Faculty Age Projection: Normal Distribution Assuming Normal Retirement at Age 70

FIVE YEAR SUMMARY AT 1998

POPULATION TABLE

AGE COHORT	BASE POPULATION	OUTMI- GRANTS	TENURE DENIALS	RECENT RETIREES	MID-CAREER CHANGE	RECENT HIRES	NET CHANGE
70 PLUS	48.	0.	0.	42.	0.	0.	-42.
65 – 69	92.	0.	0.	26.	0.	0.	-26.
60 – 64	110.	0.	0.	9.	0.	0.	-9.
55 – 59	150.	0.	0.	12.	0.	2.	-11.
50 – 54	128.	2.	0.	7.	0.	4.	-5.
45 – 49	111.	3.	0.	4.	0.	8.	0.
40 – 44	94.	7.	0.	2.	0.	19.	10.
35 – 39	85.	12.	15.	1.	0.	25.	-3.
30 – 34	113.	14.	22.	1.	0.	61.	24.
UNDER 30	69.	10.	0.	1.	0.	73.	62.
TOTAL	1000.					73.	0.

POPULATION HISTOGRAM

RESULTING POPULATION	AGE COHORT	HISTOGRAM
72.	70 PLUS	AAAAAAA
101.	65 – 69	AAAAAAAAAA
137.	60 – 64	AAAAAAAAAAAAAA
121.	55 – 59	AAAAAAAAAAAA
107.	50 – 54	AAAAAAAAAAA
92.	45 – 49	AAAAAAAAA
76.	40 – 44	AAAAAAAA
100.	35 – 39	AAAAAAAAAA
119.	30 – 34	AAAAAAAAAAAA
73.	UNDER 30	AAAAAAA
1000.	TOTAL	

Figure 12d

Faculty Age Projection: Normal Distribution Assuming Normal Retirement at Age 65

FIVE YEAR SUMMARY AT 2008

POPULATION TABLE

AGE COHORT	BASE POPULATION	OUTMI- GRANTS	TENURE DENIALS	RECENT RETIREES	MID-CAREER CHANGE	RECENT HIRES	NET CHANGE
70 PLUS	10.	0.	0.	10.	0.	0.	-10.
65 - 69	98.	0.	0.	86.	0.	0.	-86.
60 - 64	115.	0.	0.	33.	0.	0.	-33.
55 - 59	108.	0.	0.	9.	0.	3.	-7.
50 - 54	103.	2.	0.	5.	0.	5.	-2.
45 - 49	94.	3.	0.	3.	0.	10.	3.
40 - 44	106.	7.	0.	3.	0.	25.	15.
35 - 39	127.	12.	19.	2.	0.	33.	-1.
30 - 34	149.	14.	29.	2.	0.	81.	36.
UNDER 30	90.	10.	0.	1.	0.	96.	85.
TOTAL	1000.						0.

POPULATION HISTOGRAM

POPULATION HISTOGRAM	RESULTING POPULATION	AGE COHORT
A	13.	70 PLUS
A AAAAAAAA	81.	65 - 69
AAAAAAAAA	98.	60 - 64
AAAAAAAAA	98.	55 - 59
AAAAAAAA	92.	50 - 54
AAAAAAAAAA	106.	45 - 49
AAAAAAAAAAA	119.	40 - 44
AAAAAAAAAAAAA	138.	35 - 39
AAAAAAAAAAAAAAA	159.	30 - 34
AAAAAAAAA	96.	UNDER 30
	1000.	TOTAL

154

Figure 13d
Faculty Age Projection: Normal Distribution Assuming Normal Retirement at Age 70

FIVE YEAR SUMMARY AT 2008

POPULATION TABLE

AGE COHORT	BASE POPULATION	OUTMI-GRANTS	TENURE DENIALS	RECENT RETIREES	MID-CAREER CHANGE	RECENT HIRES	NET CHANGE	RESULTING POPULATION	AGE COHORT
70 PLUS	81.	0.	0.	71.	0.	0.	-71.	100.	70 PLUS
65 – 69	126.	0.	0.	36.	0.	0.	-36.	102.	65 – 69
60 – 64	111.	0.	0.	9.	0.	0.	-9.	93.	60 – 64
55 – 59	102.	0.	0.	8.	0.	2.	-6.	85.	55 – 59
50 – 54	90.	2.	0.	5.	0.	5.	-2.	74.	50 – 54
45 – 49	75.	3.	0.	3.	0.	9.	3.	93.	45 – 49
40 – 44	94.	7.	0.	2.	0.	23.	13.	102.	40 – 44
35 – 39	110.	12.	17.	2.	0.	30.	-1.	120.	35 – 39
30 – 34	130.	14.	25.	1.	0.	73.	33.	144.	30 – 34
UNDER 30	81.	10.	0.	1.	0.	87.	76.	87.	UNDER 30
TOTAL	1000.						0.	1000.	TOTAL

POPULATION HISTOGRAM

```
70 PLUS    AAAAAAAAAA
65 – 69    AAAAAAAAAA
60 – 64    AAAAAAAAAA
55 – 59    AAAAAAAAA
50 – 54    AAAAAAAA
45 – 49    AAAAAAAAAA
40 – 44    AAAAAAAAAAA
35 – 39    AAAAAAAAAAAAA
30 – 34    AAAAAAAAAAAAAAAA
UNDER 30   AAAAAAAAAA
```

Figure 12e
Faculty Age Projection: Normal Distribution Assuming Normal Retirement at Age 65

FIVE YEAR SUMMARY AT 2018

POPULATION TABLE

AGE COHORT	BASE POPULATION	OUTMI-GRANTS	TENURE DENIALS	RECENT RETIRES	MID-CAREER CHANGE	RECENT HIRES	NET CHANGE	RESULTING POPULATION	AGE COHORT
70 PLUS	10.	0.	0.	10.	0.	0.	-10.	9.	70 PLUS
65 - 69	70.	0.	0.	61.	0.	0.	-61.	63.	65 - 69
60 - 64	89.	0.	0.	26.	0.	0.	-26.	80.	60 - 64
55 - 59	88.	0.	0.	7.	0.	2.	-5.	99.	55 - 59
50 - 54	104.	2.	0.	6.	0.	5.	-3.	115.	50 - 54
45 - 49	118.	3.	0.	4.	0.	9.	1.	125.	45 - 49
40 - 44	126.	7.	0.	3.	0.	23.	12.	130.	40 - 44
35 - 39	143.	12.	22.	2.	0.	29.	-7.	142.	35 - 39
30 - 34	161.	14.	33.	2.	0.	72.	24.	152.	30 - 34
UNDER 30	91.	10.	0.	1.	0.	86.	75.	86.	UNDER 30
TOTAL	1000.						0.	1000.	TOTAL

POPULATION HISTOGRAM

AGE COHORT	POPULATION	HISTOGRAM
70 PLUS	9.	A
65 - 69	63.	AAAAAA
60 - 64	80.	AAAAAAAA
55 - 59	99.	AAAAAAAAAA
50 - 54	115.	AAAAAAAAAAAA
45 - 49	125.	AAAAAAAAAAAAA
40 - 44	130.	AAAAAAAAAAAAA
35 - 39	142.	AAAAAAAAAAAAAA
30 - 34	152.	AAAAAAAAAAAAAAAA
UNDER 30	86.	AAAAAAAAA
TOTAL	1000.	

Figure 13e
Faculty Age Projection: Normal Distribution Assuming Normal Retirement at Age 70

FIVE YEAR SUMMARY AT 2018

POPULATION TABLE

AGE COHORT	BASE POPULATION	OUTMI-GRANTS	TENURE DENIALS	RECENT RETIREES	MID-CAREER CHANGE	RECENT HIRES	NET CHANGE	RESULTING POPULATION	AGE COHORT
70 PLUS	85.	0.	0.	74.	0.	0.	-74.	72.	70 PLUS
65 – 69	85.	0.	0.	24.	0.	0.	-24.	71.	65 – 69
60 – 64	78.	0.	0.	6.	0.	0.	-7.	64.	60 – 64
55 – 59	70.	0.	0.	6.	0.	2.	-4.	87.	55 – 59
50 – 54	91.	2.	0.	5.	0.	5.	-2.	99.	50 – 54
45 – 49	102.	3.	0.	4.	0.	9.	2.	110.	45 – 49
40 – 44	111.	7.	0.	3.	0.	23.	13.	121.	40 – 44
35 – 39	132.	12.	20.	2.	0.	29.	-4.	137.	35 – 39
30 – 34	153.	14.	30.	2.	0.	72.	27.	153.	30 – 34
UNDER 30	91.	10.	0.	1.	0.	86.	75.	86.	UNDER 30
TOTAL	1000.						0.	1000.	TOTAL

POPULATION HISTOGRAM

```
70 PLUS     AAAAAAA
            AAAAAAA
65 – 69     AAAAAAA
            AAAAAAA
60 – 64     AAAAAA
            AAAAAA
55 – 59     AAAAAAAAA
            AAAAAAAAA
50 – 54     AAAAAAAAAA
            AAAAAAAAAA
45 – 49     AAAAAAAAAAA
            AAAAAAAAAAA
40 – 44     AAAAAAAAAAAA
            AAAAAAAAAAAA
35 – 39     AAAAAAAAAAAAAA
            AAAAAAAAAAAAAA
30 – 34     AAAAAAAAAAAAAAAA
            AAAAAAAAAAAAAAAA
UNDER 30    AAAAAAAAA
            AAAAAAAAA
```

the reduction is 10%. During the next decade the reduction varies from year to year because a bimodal age distribution develops. Average five-year reductions during these years vary between 14% and 22%. However, by the thirtieth year the rates begin to converge, and by the thirty-fifth year new-appointment rates are identical.

It is important to remember that these reductions are estimates based on the assumption that all faculty members planning to retire at or above age 60 would postpone their retirement five years. It is, however, reasonable to assume that not all faculty members will retire at older ages now that the mandatory retirement age has been raised, nor would all who would postpone their retirements do so for a full five years. Thus, we expect the reduction in openings for new employees would be less than we have shown here.

Although the long-term impact of an increase in the average age at retirement might be negligible, some institutions might not be able to weather the transition, even if the reduction were only 10%. Indeed, there may be serious near-term problems for specific institutions. Even if the percentage of persons postponing their retirements were not as great as we assume here, some decline in the retirement rate during the five to ten years following the abolition of mandatory retirement would be likely. This fact recommends the policy of inducing early retirements during this transition period in order to offset the decrease in the retirement rate brought about by postponed retirements. The extent of the inducement should depend on local conditions, including the age structure of the faculty and the percentage of persons who plan to opt for a later retirement age.

Possible Changes in the Model

The model is intended to describe changes in the distribution of faculty members using rates and distributions describing academia in general. For a specific institution, another model—one dealing with one-year age groups, years-to-tenure rates, promotion rates, and other variables—would be more appropriate. Our model was developed to analyze the results of different combinations of rates and to test the effect of various policies on typical population distributions. Models requiring institution-specific data have been developed, and any institution considering early-retirement options should analyze its options with such a model. At least one model is available to interested organizations. The University of Southern California Faculty Flow Model—available from the Office of Institutional Studies, University of Southern California—was developed by Dr. Paul Grey.[7] His model is based on individual cases, as opposed to age-cohort distributions of faculty. Instead of using a tenure-denial rate, it uses a probability distribution for the determination of tenure and thus requires a record of tenure history. The model is applicable to schools with faculties of up to 250 persons.

A model developed by David S. P. Hopkins projects changes in the age cohorts of the faculty using a Markov-chain process.[8] The model requires rates from historical data.

A linear programming model developed by R. G. Schroeder also uses faculty age cohorts in making projections.[9] This model's inputs include student course demand, which is reflected in the number of faculty members annually needed to teach in that particular field.

Interested institutions should examine these models and adapt them to their specific needs.

IMPLICATIONS

The analysis indicates that tenure-denial and outmigration are the most sensitive rates. The others—mid-career change, death, retirement, and the distributions among the cohorts for new hires and outmigration—should be thought of as "fine-tuning" in the effort to obtain a particular faculty population distribution.

Administrators are reminded that although a model with properly selected rates yields a particular population, other factors must be considered. For example, how can an institution realistically obtain a 20% death and retirement rate in the 60-to-64 age cohort? Since it cannot control the death rate, a system of incentives would have to be established to make retirement an attractive alternative for almost 20% of that age cohort. This involves not only a policy change but financial planning. A university cannot afford to make a wrong decision concerning the cost of such a policy. True, manipulating the rates can yield just about any population distribution an institution desires, but whether these rates can be obtained in practice is another question.

Since the tenure-denial rate is the most sensitive rate, an administrator might conclude that by increasing the tenure denials he could bring about a desired population distribution. However, when the tenure-denial rate is increased to a high level, the population takes on a bimodal distribution. Intuitively, this does not seem to be a desirable manpower distribution. An institution might not consider a high tenure-denial rate if it also would discourage faculty members from joining the university. Yet going to the other extreme and choosing a low tenure-denial rate is not the right approach either, for that would clearly reduce the number of new appointments that could be made.[10]

In practice, too few faculty members are affected by a policy that banks on high retirement rates. Even in institutions where cost is no object, it may be difficult to obtain high rates of retirement.

The mid-career change rate may work well for institutions that want to reduce the number of faculty members approaching the near-retirement years. However, we were unable to locate any programs that induce substantial mid-career change. Although manipulation of mid-career change rates is possible in our model, in practice—even in an effective program—it may be difficult to obtain the rates we used.

NOTES

1. David Palmer, "Basic Age Distributions by Field by Type of Institution," mimeo. (Storrs, Conn.: University of Connecticut, School of Business Administration, 20 October, 1976). The Carnegie Council age distributions were drawn from the Carnegie survey data tape by Mark Aarens of the University of California Survey Research Center.

2. The Carnegie survey classifies institutions by both type and quality. The institutions sampled are classified first by the degree they award, thereby distinguishing among universities, four-year colleges, and junior colleges. Then the universities and four-year colleges are assigned to quality categories determined by the characteristics and qualifications of students and faculty and by institutional resources. See Martin A. Trow, *Technical Report: Carnegie Commission National Survey of Higher Education* (Berkeley: Carnegie Commission on Higher Education, 1972).

3. Frank J. Atelsek and Irene L. Gomberg, *Young Doctorate Faculty in Selected Science and Engineering Departments, 1975 to 1980* (Washington, D.C.: American Council on Education, 1976).

4. Robert K. Foertsch developed the faculty flow model and wrote the first draft of this section of the chapter.

5. Paul Grey, "College and University Planning Models," mimeo. (Los Angeles: University of Southern California, Office of Institutional Studies, January 1976); David S. P. Hopkins, "Faculty Early Retirement Programs," *Operations Research* 22, no. 3 (1974): 455–467; David S. P.

Hopkins, "Analysis of Faculty Appointment, Promotion, and Retirement Policies," *Higher Education* 3, no. 4 (November 1974): 397–418; and R. G. Schroeder, "Resource Planning in University Management by Goal Programming," *Operations Research* 22 (July/August 1974): 700–710.

6. Allan M. Cartter and John M. McDowell, "Projected Market and Institutional Policy Impact on Faculty Composition," mimeo. (Los Angeles: Univeristy of California, Department of Higher Education, February 1975); and Albert H. Bowker, *Berkeley in a Steady State,* mimeo. (Berkeley: University of California, Office of the Chancellor, 21 September 1973).

7. Grey, "Planning Models."

8. Hopkins, "Faculty Early Retirement Programs" and "Analysis of Faculty Appointment, Promotion and Retirement Policies."

9. Schroeder, "Resource Planning."

10. David Katz has developed and will make available on request, a model which can be used to project the tenure ratio when faculty size is constant. Two difference equations are used to project the tenure ratio under various assumptions of positive or negative growth, retirements and resignations, promotions and new hires. See David A. Katz, "Tenure Ratios under Conditions of Positive or Negative Faculty Growth," *AAUP Bulletin* 63, no. 4 (November 1977): 301–303.

6

Legal Questions Concerning Early Retirement[1]

In recent years federal legislation and court decisions have modified retirement plans and practices. Because of, and in spite of, these influences, ambiguity surrounds the legal issues in the retirement of college and university faculty members. Public and private institutions are affected differently by the legislation, and the number of questions that remain unanswered warrants caution in making assumptions about the applicability of specific provisions of the law to particular programs and institutions. Nevertheless, several issues about the funding of pension programs and questions about possible discrimination should be recognized by institutions considering induced early-retirement options.

FUNDING REQUIREMENTS AND TAX IMPLICATIONS

The Employee Retirement Income Security Act of 1974 (ERISA) was passed to protect the pension rights of employees.[2] Generally, ERISA places a number of statutory controls on all present and future private pension plans. Employees are guaranteed accrued benefits after a minimum number of years of participation. The law requires that the plans be adequately funded to pay the benefits, that the pension funds be prudently managed, and that certain plan benefits be insured. Other provisions place ceilings on contributions to certain plans and on benefits from other plans. Requirements for reporting to government agencies and for disclosure of information to plan participants and beneficiaries are specified.

Most private employee retirement plans are regulated by the provisions of ERISA. Supplemental plans for individual employees are not. It is this latter category in which we are primarily interested, since supplemental plans may be used to make early retirement more attractive to certain employees. To understand the implications of these plans, it is necessary to consider how pension plans are generally affected by the tax laws.

Qualified Pension Plans. Pension plans that meet Internal Revenue Service requirements as to non-discrimination and funding are known as "qualified" plans because they qualify for certain tax advantages which accrue to employers and employees.

The amounts contributed by an employer to a qualified pension or other deferred compensation plan are deductible on the employer's income tax return for that year. Of course the employer receives deductions for other types of compensation paid to employees as ordinary and necessary business expenses. With a qualified plan, the employer receives the deduction for contributing funds to the plan even though the employees receive no benefits from the plan that year. Thus, the employer may accumulate deferred compensation for employees and at the same time suffer no current tax disadvantage.

The employees under a qualified plan are taxed only when they actually receive their benefit payments or when the funds are made available to them. If received upon retirement or termination of employment, a large amount may be taxable not at current income tax rates but at the lower long-term capital-gains rates. That portion not eligible for capital-gains treatment may qualify for ten-year forward income-averaging.

At death, the amount in an employee's account attributable to employer contributions can pass to a beneficiary (other than an estate) free of estate tax. And the first $5,000 of the death benefit from a deceased employee's account (attributable to employer contributions) can go to his beneficiary free of income tax. Of course, the employee recovers his contributions tax-free. Furthermore, an employee with a vested interest in a qualified plan usually need not pay any gift tax when he irrevocably designates a beneficiary to receive payments at his death. This tax break is restricted to the survivorship interest attributable to employer contributions.

The basic requirements for pension plan qualification were generally increased by ERISA. To qualify, the terms of the plan must be set forth in writing, and the plan must be intended as permanent and continuing. The assets of the plan must be kept separate from those of the plan sponsor (employer or employee organization) so that the plan is operated for the exclusive benefit of the participants and beneficiaries. The plan must benefit employees in general and not merely a limited number of favored employees; a qualified pension plan may not discriminate in favor of officers, shareholders, and highly compensated employees as to coverage, contributions, or benefits.

Nonqualified Pension Plans. Most pension plans that do not meet IRS requirements for qualified plans were also affected by the passage of ERISA. In contrast to Title II, which amends the Internal Revenue Code of 1954 relating primarily to qualified pension plans, Title I applies to most employee pension and welfare-benefit plans, whether qualified or not.[3] Title I, known as "the Labor regulatory provisions," is concerned with the protection of employee benefit rights. It covers participation, vesting, funding, reporting and disclosure, fiduciary responsibility, and enforcement of rights. In many respects, these provisions are essentially the same as the IRS requirements for pension plan qualification. However, the Labor Department has provided little guidance on coverage of nonqualified plans under ERISA.

An employer gets no deduction for a contribution to a nonqualified plan until the employee includes that contribution in his gross income. Generally, the employee need not report the income on his tax return until his right to the money is nonforfeitable. The benefits will be deemed forfeitable if the employee must continue on the job to receive them.

An employer might provide benefits to certain employees through an excess-benefit plan. ERISA Sec 3(36) defines this arrangement as a plan maintained by an employer solely for the purpose of providing benefits for certain employees in excess of limitations imposed by Section 415 of the Internal Revenue Code, regardless of whether the plan is funded.[4] Funded excess-benefit plans (those in which funds are placed in trust or out of reach of the employer) are subject to ERISA, but they are rare. Unfunded excess-benefit plans (those in which benefits are paid from the general assets of the employer) are excluded from ERISA coverage on the grounds that employees who benefit from such plans need little, if any, protection by the law. Since the plans are unfunded, there are few fiduciary problems.

On many occasions a nonqualified, funded, excess-benefits plan might fit in with an employer's policies. The employer is able to pick and choose among the benefit levels and employees who will benefit; he can supplement the benefits of a qualified plan for handpicked employees; he need not treat all employees alike, always keeping in mind that only employees may benefit. Nonqualified arrangements can be made particularly attractive if the employer is willing to defer his tax deductions until the employee receives benefits from the plan.

As an alternative to establishing a trust, an employer may finance a funded excess-benefits plan by buying an insurance contract to assure that the payment will be made. The proceeds are paid to the employer, not the employee, and the employer does not receive a deduction when the premiums are paid. However, the proceeds are nontaxable when received, and the employer is able to deduct the amount paid out to the employee. The payments are, of course, taxable to the employee when he receives them.

Annuity Plans for Tax-Exempt Institutions. Qualification or nonqualification of pension plans becomes less important for many colleges and universities that are tax-exempt under Section 501(c)(3) of the Internal Revenue Code. Under Section 403(b) of the Code, employees of tax-exempt educational institutions may exclude from their current gross income amounts paid by their employer into a custodial account or toward the purchase of an annuity. The employees' rights must be nonforfeitable, and the annuity must not be subject to the provisions of Section 403(a) of the Code relating to qualified annuity plans. Previous law required the purchase of an annuity contract from an insurance company. However, ERISA permits contributions to be held in a custodial account and invested in the stock of regulated investment companies (such as mutual funds).

The yearly contributions which may be excluded from the employee's gross income must not exceed his "exclusion allowance." This allowance is equal to 20% of the employee's includable annual compensation, multiplied by his years of service, and reduced by the amounts contributed by the employer in previous years. However, ERISA added Section 415 to the Internal Revenue Code which sets some overall limits on contributions and benefits for qualified plans but provides relief for Section 403(b) plans with three alternate "catch-up" provisions. These arrangements allow higher contributions in later years to make up for lower contributions in earlier years of employment. Contributions to a Section 403(b) annuity above the exclusion allowance or the alternative "catch-up" provisions reduce the exclusion allowance and force the employee to include the excess in his gross income. The excess contribution to a Section 403(b) custodial account is subject to a 6% tax on overfunding until it is eliminated.

RETIREMENT PLANS NOT COVERED BY ERISA

Two categories of employee benefit plans exempted from ERISA coverage are "governmental" plans and unfunded "excess-benefit" plans. Various other lump-sum and annuity arrangements used to supplement early retirement income are also not covered by ERISA.

Governmental Plans. Plans established or maintained for employees by the federal government, the government of any state or political subdivision, or any agency or instrumentality of either are exempt from the provisions of ERISA. Thus, at present, any government educational institution is free of ERISA regulation of its employee benefit plans. Note, however, that pressure exists to make public employee retirement systems subject to federal regulation. Some public employee retirement systems have been qualified (or considered qualified) by IRS in order to provide tax advantages to employee participants. For example, the IRS treats the civil service retirement system as a tax-exempt trust which is part of a qualified pension plan.

Unfunded Excess-Benefit Plans. The question of whether an excess-benefit plan is funded involves a number of factors, the most important of which is whether employees under the plan have preferred status. If benefits are guaranteed or if an employee has a direct interest in an annuity or insurance contract, the plan might be considered funded and subject to ERISA.

Nevertheless, many unfunded excess-benefit plans exist without regulation by ERISA or by agencies administering ERISA. Typically, an employer agrees to pay out of current general funds the difference between a pension benefit from early or normal retirement (plus, sometimes, social security) and some stated benefit objective. The payments become taxable income to the retiree when he receives them. It would seem that unfunded excess-benefit plans might be used to provide additional pension payments to persons who retire early. An institution should retain both financial and legal counsel when designing such a scheme.

Supplemental Plans. Considerable imagination has been shown in the development of supplemental retirement income plans in colleges and universities. Methods to achieve benefits and other objectives have varied considerably. The tailoring of supplemental plans to individual and unique institutional needs has made consideration of ERISA coverage on these plans very complicated. Two such supplemental plans include gratuitous payments and severance pay plans.

Gratuitous Payments to Pre-ERISA Retirees. Prior to the enactment of ERISA on September 2, 1974, many employers supplemented the income of retired employees by voluntarily making extra payments to them. Generally, these payments were made to counter the effect of inflation on fixed pensions. Under Department of Labor regulations,[5] such payments do not constitute a pension plan and are therefore exempt from ERISA regulations if:

1. payments are made out of the general assets of the employer,
2. they are made only to employees who were separated from the service of the employer prior to September 2, 1974,
3. the payments commenced prior to September 2, 1974, and
4. each former employee receiving the payments is notified annually that the payments are gratuitous and do not constitute a pension plan.

Recently the Labor Department revised its regulations so as to permit such payments to persons who retired prior to 1977. The payments must not be part of an employee benefit plan, must not have been communicated to employees prior to their retirement, and may not be granted for more than one year at a time.

Severance Pay Plans. In April, 1976, the Department of Labor announced revised regulations expanding the definition of severance pay plans to include payments made upon separation from employment which do not exceed two years final annual compensation or extend for more than twelve months beyond retirement. The payments must come from the employer's general assets and be identified as severance pay rather than as a pension.

LEGAL ASPECTS OF AGE DISCRIMINATION

Age discrimination suits may be brought under either the Age Discrimination in Employment Act of 1967 (Public Law 90-202) or the constitutional guarantees of due process and equal protection. The Age Discrimination in Employment Act (ADEA) prohibits virtually any form of discrimination because of age in hiring, discharge, compensation, terms and conditions of employment, employment referral, or advertising.

Under the "due process" and "equal protection" clauses of the Fourteenth Amendment to the Constitution and the "due process" clause of the Fifth Amendment, employees are provided some protection against involuntary retirement. The Age Discrimination law appears to be the more promising of the two courses for persons charging an employer with discriminatory retirement practices.

THE AGE DISCRIMINATION IN EMPLOYMENT ACT

In general, a person alleging noncompliance with the ADEA need only show a "pattern" of age discrimination to shift the burden of proof to the employer, who is then required to justify the use of age as a valid indicator of job qualification. The act originally covered persons aged 40 to 65, but in 1978 Congress passed amendments that raised the cut-off age to 70. Under an exception, the amendments permit mandatory retirement of tenured college and university professors at age 65 until July 1, 1982. The law covers state and local governments, government agencies, employers of twenty or more persons engaged in commerce, employment agencies, and labor organizations. The Secretary of Labor is authorized to conduct investigations, issue rules and regulations, and bring court action when voluntary compliance cannot be obtained.

The raising of the mandatory retirement age from 65 to 70 will undoubtedly raise questions about the conditions under which persons may be retired prior to age 70. When the mandatory age was 65, the courts decided a number of cases dealing with the involuntary retirement of persons before the mandatory age. These cases are instructive since they illustrate the difficulty the courts have had in determining the conditions under which an involuntary retirement is considered illegal, and they encouraged Congress to amend the subsection of the act dealing with involuntary retirement under the terms of a *bona fide* seniority system or benefit plan.

A case brought under the Age Discrimination in Employment Act usually alleges a discretionary pattern which, if accepted by the court, requires the defendant-employer to justify the practice at issue by demonstrating that it is not prejudicial. For example, in the case of *Schulz* v. *Hickok,* a 56-year-old district sales manager was one of seven managers discharged by Hickok during an eighteen-month period.[6] During this period, the average age of the district sales managers declined from 53 to 40. Hickok contended that it was attempting to revitalize its management force and that the sales manager was only an average producer. The court held that a *prima facie* case (one that can be overcome only by contrary evidence) had been established. The sales manager was awarded damages and reinstated.

In *Wilson* v. *Kraftco Corp.*, the fact that a 62-year-old employee who was not incompetent had been replaced by one aged 50 was enough to establish a *prima facie* case.[7] The court found that a *prima facie* case is established when the plaintiff shows:

1. membership within the protected class,
2. involuntary retirement,
3. apparently satisfactory job performance, and
4. replacement by a younger person.

In 1975, one appellate court held that an employee may recover damages even if age is only one of several factors involved in his discharge.[8] However, *in Mastie* v. *Great Lakes Steel Corporation,* a federal district court decided that age bias, unlike race or sex discrimination, requires proof that age was the determining factor in the employer's action, not simply one of many factors.[9]

In the latter case, the employer had found it necessary to reduce his work force and, therefore, induced two foremen in their late fifties to retire early. The foremen claimed age discrimination and contended that the employer saved money by discharging them instead of younger workers who earned less in salary and pension benefits. The court said, "Both the legislative history and the Department of Labor regulations tend to support the proposition that higher labor costs associated with the employment of older employees constitute 'reasonable factors other than age' than an employer can consider when faced with possible termination of an older employee."

The necessity to reduce labor costs, however, may not justify early involuntary retirement of an employer's oldest worker(s) unless age is shown to be a *bona fide* occupational qualification. In *Houghton* v. *McDonnell*, the U.S. Supreme Court recently let stand the appellate court ruling to that effect.[10]

In that case, the chief production test pilot for McDonnell Douglas was discharged when the company decided to reduce its number of test pilots. McDonnell admitted that age was the sole determinant in its decision to let Houghton go first. Houghton, then 52, was the oldest of the company's test pilots. The district court agreed with the company's claim that age is a *bona fide* occupational qualification for test pilots. But the appeals court reversed the decision, saying that since the company admitted that it let Houghton go only because of his age, the burden was on the company to prove that age was a *bona fide* occupational qualification for test pilots. Section 4(f)(1) of the Age Discrimination in Employment Act says that an employer may discriminate if he proves that age is a real test of a worker's ability to perform the job.

The company contended that aging traits in the general population would affect the performance of test pilots. Houghton, however, presented evidence that test pilots age differently than the general population and, in fact, their performance improves with age. The court, therefore, ruled that the company failed to prove that age was a *bona fide* occupational qualification.[11]

It is clear that an employer cannot discharge an employee simply because of his age. Pursuant to a consent decree between the Department of Labor and the Standard Oil Company of California, a subsidiary of Standard Oil paid approximately $2,000,000 to one hundred sixty former employees who were discharged simply because of their age.[12] In another case, the heirs of an Exxon Research and Engineering Company chemist found by a federal district court to have been forceably retired at 60 were granted a cash settlement.[13] In another court case, the Labor Department is seeking payments for three hundred employees of the Baltimore and Ohio Railroad and the Chesapeake and Ohio Railway who were forced to retire before age 65.[14]

These cases notwithstanding, an exception in the act permits differentiation based on "reasonable factors other than age," as in the *Mastie* case above. William Hamblin suggests that an employer may be able to overcome an initial statistical suggestion of discrimination if he is able to substantiate the existence and use of objective evaluative criteria.[15] In educational institutions, as in other organizations, higher salaries are generally paid to older, more experienced, persons. However, it would seem prudent not to rely solely on the proposition that higher labor costs constitute reasonable factors other than age; objective evaluative criteria should be used. But, as a further caveat, Hamblin cautions that "if an educational institution should suddenly tighten up its standards, and it can be shown that one important factor was financial (as related to years of service), then a faculty member who is being dismissed and who is within the age range covered by the act may be able to successfully allege a violation constituting age discrimination."[16] Hamblin's warning takes on added strength in light of the McDonnell Douglas test pilot case.

Until the 1978 amendment of the ADEA, Section 4 (f) (2) of the act provided for differentiation in order to observe the terms of a *bona fide* seniority system or benefit plan. An interpretive regulation of the Department of Labor seemed to authorize involuntary early retirement regardless of age if the retirement is pursuant to an acceptable overall plan. Many courts have found involuntary retirement programs unacceptable for other reasons. But in 1976 the federal district court for Hawaii took the position that the Hawaiian Telephone Company could force employees to retire early because such action was part of the terms of a *bona fide* retirement plan that would provide involuntary retirees with "substantial benefits."

The court cited the exception in the Act which then provided that it is not unlawful for an employer to observe the terms of any *bona fide* employee benefit plan that is not a subterfuge to evade the purposes of the law. The court rejected the telephone company's reliance on *Brennan* v. *Taft Broadcasting Co.*, a 1974 decision in which the Fifth Circuit Court of Appeals held that any *bona fide* plan in effect prior to the Age Discrimination in Employment Act was automatically not a "subterfuge."[17] The District Court for Hawaii said all *bona fide* plans in effect prior to the Act were not automatically "grandfathered." The court decided that the word "subterfuge" as used in the Act is applicable only if the employer "uses a retirement plan as a subterfuge to retire an employee without the payment of substantial benefits." The court concluded that the $120,000 received by the eight retirees in the short time between retirement and the court action constituted substantial benefits.[18]

A similar argument was made the following year by the Third Circuit Court of Appeals. In *Zinger* v. *Blanchette* the court distinguished between discharge and mandatory retirement on a pension, holding that there was no statutory prohibition against retirement on a pension, and that if the retirement benefits were substantial, the involuntary retirement would not be a subterfuge to evade the purposes of the act.[19]

In a comparable case, an employee was retired at age 60 from United Airlines. McMann voluntarily joined United Airline's retirement plan in 1964. It required retirement at age 60. The District Court granted a motion for summary judgment, agreeing with United that McMann was retired in compliance with the provisions of a *bona fide* retirement plan which he voluntarily joined. The Fourth Circuit Court of Appeals reversed this ruling, arguing that the mandatory retirement-at-60 provision fell within the meaning of "subterfuge" in the Age Discrimination

Act. The court held that Section 4(f) (2) did not permit mandatory retirement pursuant to the terms of a pension plan. To rule otherwise, said the court, would undermine the intent of Congress because Section 4(f) (2) was intended to encourage the employment of older workers by not requiring employers to provide them the same pension benefits as provided to other workers.[20] The court remanded the case to the District Court to provide United the opportunity to show other valid defenses for its action.

United sought review by the Supreme Court, which ruled that since the retirement plan predated the Age Discrimination Act, it was not a subterfuge. However, in both a concurring and a dissenting opinion, the fact that the retirement plan was adopted prior to the Age Discrimination Act was questioned. Justice White held that McMann's retirement was valid not because the retirement plan predated the act but because the act does not prohibit involuntary retirements pursuant to *bona fide* plans. Justices Marshall and Brennan argued that the court gave "an unduly narrow interpretation to a congressional enactment designed to remedy arbitrary discrimination in the workplace." The justices argued further that the ADEA amendments, then pending final passage, would provide that involuntary retirement not be permitted under any employee benefit plan.

The conflicting interpretations of Section 4(f) (2) led Congress to rewrite that section as part of the 1978 ADEA amendments. The Senate Human Resources Committee's report on the ADEA amendments bill argued that raising the act's upper age limit would be meaningless if employees were still subject to mandatory retirement because of provisions contained in collective bargaining agreements or employee benefit plans. The committee stated it believed that the Fourth Circuit Court had reached the proper conclusion in *McMann* and the amendment to Section 4(f) (2) would serve to express Congressional approval of the Court's results.[21]

The intent of the ADEA amendments is to prohibit the involuntary retirement of employees merely on the basis of age. This should not be read to imply that all involuntary retirements are prohibited. As noted above, Section 4(f) (1) permits involuntary retirement where age is a *bona fide* occupational qualification, and Section 4(f) (3) permits the discharging of an employee for good reason. Furthermore, Section 12(c) (1) permits compulsory retirement of an employee aged 65 or above who is employed in a *bona fide* executive or high policy making position, if that person has occupied that position for at least two years before being involuntarily retired and if he is entitled to an immediate annual retirement benefit of at least $27,000.

The ADEA amendments appear to resolve, at least temporarily, questions about the conditions under which an employee may be involuntarily retired. However, the act requires the Secretary of Labor to conduct a study of the effects of the amendments, and to prepare reports on the impact of raising the mandatory age to 70, the feasibility of eliminating the mandatory age or raising it above 70, the effect of the exemption relating to certain executive employees and the effect of the exemption for tenured teaching personnel.

It may be possible for universities and colleges to provide imaginative benefit programs which will encourage employees to voluntarily retire early. However, voluntary early retirement tied to increased benefits is not addressed in the ADEA and has not been brought before the courts. It would seem prudent for an institution to obtain legal counsel before offering an employee an increased-benefits early retirement.

CONSTITUTIONAL GUARANTEES

In addition to the Age Discrimination in Employment Act, the courts have afforded some protection against involuntary retirement by applying the "due process" and "equal protection" clauses of the Fourteenth Amendment and the "due process" clause of the Fifth Amendment to the Constitution.

In order to invoke these guarantees, the complainant must show that some governmental action is involved. Obviously, faculty members of state educational institutions could show state action. Faculty members at private educational institutions would need to show some public service, such as performance of studies under government grants or the provision of certain training which the state might otherwise be required to provide, in order to assert a cause of action under the amendments. In the 1974 case of Roberts v. Catholic University of America, the United States District Court for the District of Columbia found a professor who was forced to retire at 65 unable to maintain an action for breach of contract against the employer university. There was insufficient federal government involvement in the operation of the university to provide the professor with the basis to claim rights provided by the Constitution.[22] The court relied on an earlier ruling that there must be an influence on policy or decision making, rather than financial or tax aid, to constitute governmental involvement.

Most of the cases stressing a due process argument are based on the alleged unconstitutionality of an "irrebuttable presumption" that employees are incapable of working productively beyond a certain mandatory retirement age. There is some support for the thesis that age discrimination in employment involves a "fundamental" right. But the Supreme Court has thus far avoided considering the substantive issues involved in mandatory retirement laws and provisions.

Equal protection arguments relating to age discrimination may be heard if the court decides that age should be designated as a "suspect class." This term has been used to describe classifications such as race and national origin which are considered inherently suspect for discriminatory purposes.[23] If the Court does designate age as "suspect class," it will apply a "strict scrutiny" test of the challenged law or regulation to determine whether there has been a violation of the equal protection clause. The legislative or regulatory matter under scrutiny would have to withstand a "compelling state interest" characteristic (e.g., involving public health or safety as opposed to economic or administrative considerations) in order to be sustained. If the Court does not designate age as "suspect," the test of discrimination reverts to examination of whether the law or regulation has a "rational basis." The "rational basis" test essentially means that the Court notes whether the purposes of the legislative or regulatory matter are legitimate and whether the means to achieve them are reasonably related to the ends being sought.

In mid-1976, the Supreme Court upheld the validity of a Massachusetts statute requiring retirement of uniformed state police officers at age 50. In *Massachusetts Board of Retirement et al.* v. *Murgia,* it stated that the statute does not violate the equal protection clause of the Constitution. The Court found no need to subject the statute to strict scrutiny because governmental employment is not a fundamental right and age is not a suspect class. The Court applied the "rational basis" test and found the statute rationally related to Massachusetts' objective of protecting the public by assuring the physical preparedness of its state police force.[24]

Two other cases involving public employees resulted in rulings favoring mandatory retirement. In *Weisbrod* v. *Lynn*, an attorney with a federal agency asked the court to invalidate federal regulations requiring him to retire at age 70.[25] Although he was physically capable of carrying out his job and his performance was above average, his mandatory retirement was upheld. In another case, a Louisiana statute requiring civil-service employees to retire at 65 was upheld.[26] In these cases, as well as in the *Murgia* case, the Supreme Court held that the government agencies had a rational basis for enforcing retirement at the specified age because the ages were fairly and substantially related to maintaining an effective work force and providing for the promotion of younger employees.

Closer to the topic of this book, in early 1976 the Hawaiian Supreme Court found the University of Hawaii's retirement policy unconstitutional when subjected to a "strict scrutiny" test. A college professor was hired by a branch of the university when he was 55, obtained tenure after three years, and in 1972 was denied continued employment on reaching age 65. The retirement policy adopted by the Board of Regents permitted a person over 65 to continue appointment on the faculty if "it is demonstrated that his services are needed by the university and that he is more competent for the position than any other person available." Such appointments were renewable annually but not beyond age 70. The professor was recommended by his department colleagues for continued employment after they screened forty-five applicants and found him more competent. But the chancellor denied the reappointment on the basis that a replacement was available.

The professor sued, and the district court found that, although age ceilings for retirement are not prohibited *per se* under equal protection analysis, the mandatory retirement policy in question could not withstand strict judicial scrutiny in light of the "fundamental right to public employment." The court noted the similarity to *Massachusetts Board of Retirement* v. *Murgia,* which was then pending Supreme Court review, but found the professor's case easier to decide since the Hawaiian legislature (in the context of employment) had declared age to be a suspect class. The court rejected the university's arguments that the reappointment procedure was a proper means of preserving the state's funds by paying lower salaries to younger, less experienced persons, and that it was a means of building morale among the younger faculty members. The court said the "inevitable relationship" between age and the ability to perform work did not justify the university's action.[27]

More recently, a teacher in Illinois claimed that mandatory retirement at age 65 violated his constitutional right not to be discriminated against. The Seventh Court of Appeals ruled that Illinois must prove there is a "rational basis" for its law requiring the retirement of teachers at age 65.[28] The Court said that no evidence had been presented to show that forcing teachers to retire at age 65 accomplishes any legitimate purpose. The case was sent back to the district court to give the state the opportunity to prove that its regulation is necessary. The outcome of this case will undoubtedly be affected by the boosting of the mandatory retirement age to 70.

The state of the law, as must be obvious by now, is applicable to a wide variety of situations. The ADEA amendments have resolved some of the issues surrounding the involuntary retirement of employees, but new issues are certain to arise. There is already pressure to raise the mandatory age even higher or eliminate it entirely, and the exemptions for certain business executives and the temporary exemption for tenured teachers are being questioned.

By delaying the application of the amendments to tenured teachers until 1982, Congress recognized the current manpower problem in colleges and universities. These four years will give universities time to prepare for the higher mandatory retirement age. However, the long run need is to develop objective measures to evaluate the performance of professors since chronological age is not a sufficient measure of ability and effectiveness.

Whether increased-benefits early retirement options will be challenged as violating the ADEA or the "due process" and "equal protection" amendments to the Constitution is uncertain. This would depend, it seems, upon whether these types of retirements are seen as truly voluntary. In the situations we examined, apparently professors are not being forced to accept increased-benefits early retirement, although several reported feeling that they had few alternatives, especially those who had lost interest in teaching or felt that their performance had declined.

Little more can be said than that educational institutions must exercise extreme care in designing and offering increased-benefits early retirement. It goes without saying that an institution considering the adoption of such an option should obtain legal counsel and attend to changes in the Age Discrimination in Employment Act.

NOTES

1. The initial draft of this chapter was written by Robert Lake. Susan E. Rees updated the survey of cases and suggested modifications in the text.

2. The Employee Retirement Income Security Act defines the terms "employee pension benefit plan" and "pension plan" to mean "any plan, fund or program . . . established or maintained by an employer or by an employee organization, or by both, to the extent that by its express terms or

as a result of surrounding circumstances such plan, fund, or program . . . provides retirement income to employees or results in a deferral of income by employees for periods extending to the termination of employment or beyond, regardless of the method of calculating the benefits under the plan or the method of distributing benefits from the plan." ERISA Sec. 3(2).

3. This applies to plans established or maintained by employers engaged in interstate commerce and by employee organizations representing employees engaged in interstate commerce. ERISA Sec. 3(11).

4. A plan is *funded* if funds have been placed in trust or otherwise put beyond the reach of the employer in order to assure that the means to pay accrued benefits will be available. A plan is *unfunded* if no funds are put aside to pay obligations made to prospective beneficiaries. It is understood that payments to be made will be funded when they fall due.

5. Regulation 29 CFR Section 2510.3-2(e), *(Federal Register,* 15 August 1975, vol. 40, no. 159).

6. *Schulz* v. *Hickok,* 358 F. Supp. 1208 (N.D.C. 1973).

7. *Wilson* v. *Kraftco Corp.,* 501 F. 2d 84 (5th Cir. 1974).

8. *Laugeson* v. *Anaconda Co.,* 510 F. 2d 307 (6th Cir. 1975).

9. *Matsie, et al.* v. *Great Lakes Steel Corp.,* U.S.D.E. Mich., No. 38681, 20 December 1976.

10. U.S. Sup. Ct., No. 77-309, 28 November 1977.

11. *Houghton* v. *McDonnell Douglas Corp.,* 553 F. 2d 516 (8th Cir., 20 April 1977).

12. U.S.D.L. 74-248, 16 May 1974.

13. *Rogers* v. *Exxon Research and Engineering Co.,* 550 F. 2d. 834 (3rd Cir., 20 January 1977).

14. J. Roger O'Meara, *Retirement: Reward or Rejection?* (New York: The Conference Board, 1977), p. 32.

15. William H. Hamblin, "Mandatory Retirement and Dismissal in Institutions of Higher Education—Legal Considerations Related to Age Discrimination," mimeo. (Los Angeles: University of Southern California, Office of Institutional Studies, 1976), p. 6.

16. Hamblin, "Mandatory Retirement and Dismissal," p. 9.

17. *Brennan* v. *Taft Broadcasting Co.,* 500 F. 2d. 212 (5th Cir., 1974).

18. *Dunlop* v. *Hawaiian Telephone Co.,* 415 F. Supp. 380, U.S.D.C., Hawaii, No. 75-293, 23 June 1976.

19. *Zinger* v. *Blanchette,* 549 F.2d. 901 (3rd Cir., 1977).

20. *United Arlines* v. *McMann*, U.S. Sup. Ct., No. 76-906, 12 December 1977.

21. U.S. Congress, Senate, Human Resources Committee. *Senate Report No. 95-493* [to accompany H.R. 5383, Age Discrimination in Employment Act Amendments of 1978], 12 October 1977.

22. *Roberts* v. *Catholic University of America,* District of Columbia, 1974.

23. *Frontiero* v. *Richardson,* 93 S. Ct. 1964, 1973.

24. *Massachusetts Board of Retirement et al.* v. *Murgia.,* S. Ct. No. 74-1044, 25 June 1976.

25. *Weisbrod* v. *Lynn,* No. 74-594, 15 November 1974.

26. J. Roger O'Meara, "Retirement," *Across the Board* 14, no. 1 (January 1977): 4-8.

27. *Nelson* v. *Miwa, et al.,* Hawaii, No. 5560, 24 February 1976.

28. *Gault* v. *Garrison,* No. 74-1579, 20 December 1977.

7

Conclusion

THE PROMISE OF CAREER OPTIONS

Early retirement's appeal has waxed and waned during the past few years. At first, early retirement was billed as a way to save money at the same time a faculty was revitalized with new, vigorous academics. In practice, institutions found they saved little money because the retiring person usually had to be replaced, and in some instances highly valued faculty members left. When these problems were reported, some institutions decided not to implement increased-benefits early retirement. The forthcoming increase in the mandatory retirement age for academics has caused a reconsideration of increased-benefits early retirement as a way to offset the effect of postponed retirements. If changes in the mandatory-retirement laws cause academics to delay retirement, there will be a decrease in the number of positions for new faculty members in the near-term. Increased-benefits early retirement might be used to encourage a few people to retire rather than to stay on to accumulate larger pensions.

Numerous institutions, both public and private, inside and outside of academia, have recognized induced early retirement as a way to encourage a few persons to retire early. These organizations have found that by carefully setting benefit levels, by clearly stating the terms of the early-retirement provisions, and by approaching employees in the right way, there are advantages to an increased-benefits early-retirement plan. This scheme alone has not dramatically changed the nature and composition of work forces or faculties, nor has it saved a great deal of money; but it has permitted a few important replacements during times when staffs were otherwise not increasing. At the same time, increased benefits have made it possible for some individuals who wanted to retire early (but who might not have had enough years of service for a decent pension) to obtain the financial means to do so. In a few cases, even when replacement employees were hired, the organizations saved money; but almost unanimously these organizations point out that saving money should not be the primary reason for adopting an incentive early-retirement scheme. Rather, early retirement is of special relevance to the organization wanting to make a few qualitative adjustments.

Mid-career change is another story. Few firms have programs to facilitate mid-career change for employees with higher levels of education and responsibility. Most retraining at these levels is directed at highly-valued employees whom the firm wants to retain. There is a general reluctance to make additional investments in unproductive employees who can be terminated, transferred, or encouraged to retire. Institutional programs for faculty retraining are a recent development. These, however, are not career change programs *per se,* since the retrained faculty members generally continue within the same institutions or systems, though perhaps in different departments.

Although they are potentially useful for encouraging faculty turnover, early-retirement and mid-career change programs are only two of several tools which might be used for this purpose. As the faculty flow model shows (and as the models used by others also depict), the early-retirement rate has to be boosted quite high to make much of an impact on a faculty in quantitative terms. Similarly, induced outmigration in the middle-age groups has to be several percentage points per year to permit extensive hiring of new employees. It is doubtful whether either the early-retirement or the mid-career change rates can be increased enough in practice.

Extensive turnover can be induced by reducing the rate at which tenure is granted, but there is a practical limit to the percentage of young faculty members who can be denied tenure. Although high tenure-denial rates will cause high turnover (even when faculty size is held constant), that turnover will be limited to the under-forty group. Furthermore, excessively high tenure-denial rates will likely affect the labor supply adversely. Even graduates who have the ability and drive to advance may avoid entering academia if they see tenure-denial rates set to maximize turnover.

Before jumping on the early-retirement or mid-career change bandwagon, institutions must be certain of their needs, the price they are willing to pay for turnover, and how changes in the early-retirement and mid-career change rates will affect their faculty flow. Each institution considering these options should examine its current faculty age composition by field, its tenure-granting rates, its outmigration rates, and the other factors enumerated in chapter 5. Only then can it calculate the effect of various mid-career and early-retirement options. An institution may find that its staffing problems will be ameliorated by the natural aging of the faculty during the next five to ten years. Or it may find that one of the options described in this book can be helpful and worth its cost.

MID-CAREER CHANGE OPTIONS

The vast majority of professors who choose to leave academic life for other careers do so individually, without the intervention of any formal program. Little research has been conducted on the ways in which institutions can intervene to encourage and facilitate the process. However, at least two formal routes to career change are now being used by faculty members. They are internship and fellowship programs, which provide a "visiting" experience in a new work setting, and retraining programs for continued academic work in the same institution or statewide system, albeit in a different specialty or discipline.

INTERNSHIP AND FELLOWSHIP PROGRAMS

Professors on leaves of absence have many opportunities to experiment with new kinds of work in new settings. Though the programs that support these activities are seldom explicitly directed toward career change, a substantial minority of recipients are known to remain with the organizations in which they were placed or to move to a similar organization outside the academic world. Examples of such programs are the Economic Policy Fellowships of the Brookings Institution and the Congressional Science and Engineering Fellowship Program of the American Association for the Advancement of Science. Since these programs are generally administered externally, colleges and universities have little control over the selection of appropriate grantees.

RETRAINING PROGRAMS

Retraining programs have emerged principally from the desire to reduce or abolish selected academic programs while maintaining commitments to faculty members by retraining them for work in fields which are in demand. Although such programs exist only in a few institutions, they are being planned or seriously considered by others. Because the professor continues in the same institution or system, these are not precisely career-change programs; but they do offer a college or university the flexibility to reallocate resources.

The small number of retraining programs and the limited number of participants who had completed these programs when this research was conducted combined with the program's relative newness prevents a detailed evaluation of their effectiveness. However, a number of points raised during our investigation should be considered by institutions contemplating such an option.

Nature of the Retraining Program. Care must be taken to assure that the level and scope of training will satisfy the appointee's new responsibilities. In one institution, the receiving department retained a faculty member from the same discipline at a respected neighboring institution to help design its retraining program and to act as a mediator between the retraining professor and the receiving department.

Level of Support. Existing programs provide full salary and benefits to the retrainee, plus educational and incidental expenses. One institution places a formal maximum of $3,000 on the latter, but it has exceeded this amount in special circumstances. In some cases, a replacement faculty member (usually of the most junior level) is provided to the originating department. Most of the instances of which we know concern positions slated for retrenchment. The originating department thus has less influence on the decisions than the receiving department.

Application and Decision Process. Proposals are submitted by the prospective retrainee to a screening committee. Sometimes there are committees at both the institutional and system level. Applications are often prompted by department chairmen and deans within the institution. The proposals are invariably preceded by or concurrent with negotiations establishing with certainty the existence, level, and obligations of the position that the retrainee will hold in the receiving department.

Selection and Placement Processes. These steps are sensitive to both the institution and to the individual. Experience indicates that these sensitivities are best recognized and dealt with when selection is handled by institution-wide committees with broad faculty representation.

Placement is rarely a separate process. Generally, the only candidates selected for retraining are those for whom a new placement has already been devised. Sometimes, however, details about joint appointments, courses to be taught, seniority, etc., remain to be decided even after the major decisions about retraining and placement have been made.

Other Administrative Considerations. In both of the statewide systems that we studied in detail, a person may join a department only with the consent of that department. This requirement necessitates some mechanism for negotiating retrainee transfers. In one of these statewide systems, tenure adheres to the individual within the institution and must therefore adhere to his new departmental position. Seniority, however, which is specified in the system's collective bargaining agreement, adheres to the individual within his department only. In some instances, the matter has been so difficult to resolve that the retrained faculty member has remained formally in the old department while serving either full- or part-time in his new department. Each department has been compensated for an appropriate portion of the professor's salary.

An institution considering retraining programs must be sensitive to complications arising out of its arrangements with faculty members and faculty bargaining agents. It is also realistic to expect difficulties stemming from the disciplinary and departmental modes of academic organization which might resist individuals crossing these lines in mid-career. Support, on the other hand, is likely to come from increased acceptance of faculty development as a legitimate activity of academics and of their institutions.

EARLY-RETIREMENT ALTERNATIVES

Because there has been widespread experience with incentive early-retirement options, the early-retirement schemes outlined earlier may be evaluated in more detail. They may be judged in relation to a set of criteria. Seven criteria derived during the design stage of this research project deserve attention.

Funds Freed by the Alternative. Will there be sufficient funds freed to hire replacement faculty members? For how long will these funds be available?

The Employee-Replacement Rate. Another way to express the amount of funds freed is to translate them into the number of new persons who could be hired with them. One option might free more funds per early retiree, but another option might appeal to more employees and thus free more faculty positions.

Retirement Income and Annuity Level. From the perspective of the potential early retiree, the level of the retirement annuity is perhaps the most important criterion. The level of that income can be measured in two ways: (1) the early retirement annuity as a percentage of normal retirement annuity, and (2) the early retirement annuity as a percentage of preretirement salary. Since some of the early-retirement options include a part-time employment provision, retirement income and retirement annuity income must be distinguished.

Administrative Feasibility. Administrative considerations include the possible need for changes in pension legislation or basic personnel policy before a scheme can be implemented, the identification of the source of funds to finance the plan, the delegation of authority to reallocate released funds, and so on. Are the alternatives reasonable when the age structure of the faculty is considered? In some cases there may be no age-structure problem. In other cases the normal sequence of events may correct low retirement levels.

Legal Feasibility. Any early-retirement plan must be designed with an eye to possible legal difficulties. Will the proposed alternative invite charges of discrimination from persons who feel that they are being forced to quit working because of age? Such suits could be brought against an employer under the Age Discrimination in Employment Act. How do the alternatives stand in relation to ERISA laws and to Sections 403(b) and 415 of the Internal Revenue Code? Specifically, how may the supplements be purchased and paid to the employee? What are the potential tax problems?

Political Feasibility. Institutions considering early-retirement alternatives must recognize their potential political difficulties. On the one hand, employee unions and faculty associations may react against an early-retirement provision if it appears to infringe on job security. Yet they may support early retirement as an employee benefit. Certain early-retirement options might require approval from external sources.

Market Feasibility. Options that include part-time employment provisions must also be evaluated in terms of the labor market's ability to absorb program participants. Although an early retiree may not plan to reemploy on a part-time basis, the potential availability of employment may influence his acceptance of early retirement.

Meeting the Criteria

Although each institution will have to develop its own analysis of the pros and cons of various early-retirement alternatives, a tentative evaluation of the alternatives follows. It is summarized in Table 17.

Alternative 1: Full Salary Early Annuity. This alternative frees few funds because the employee's salary is continued; although for long-term employees with substantial pension accumulations, a moderate amount of funds may be freed. This plan has a high acceptance rate. Unless money is no object, however, few employees can be replaced through it because so little money is released per retiree. The employee who retires under this option has a high income replacement level. The option is easy to administer, since the organization in essence selects people to participate. Still, there may be legal problems because of the limitation on the amount that can be added to one's pension at retirement and because the offer is made only to selected employees. There may be political problems as well, since other employees may see this arrangement as lavish payment for poor performance. The question of market feasibility does not apply, for the early retiree would not be reemployed, nor would he need to reemploy with such a substantial income.

Alternative 2: Severance Payment. This alternative often frees a sizeable portion of the early retiree's salary line because the lump-sum payment may be equivalent to only one year's pay. Larger lump-sum payments, of course, mean fewer dollars for hiring new employees. The employee replacement rate is high under this option for two reasons: (1) a substantial portion of an employee's salary line remains after this alternative is financed, and (2) the option usually appeals to a sizable number of employees. However, these persons may retire only a year or two early. This option produces a medium to low income-replacement level since one year's salary is spread over several years. The scheme is

Table 17 Summary Evaluation of Ten Early Retirement Options

Option				Criterion				
	Potential Funds Freed	Employee Replacement Rate	Retirement Income Level	Administrative Feasibility	Legal Feasibility	Political Feasibility	Market Feasibility
Full-Salary Annuity	Low	Low	High	High	Low	Low	NA
Severance Payment	Medium to High	High	Low to Medium	High	High	Medium	Medium
Individual-Based Annuity	Medium	Medium	Medium	Medium	Medium	Medium	Medium
Group-Based Annuity	Medium	Medium	Medium	Medium	Medium	Low to Medium	Medium
Partial Employment– Individual Annuity	Low to Medium	Low to Medium	High	Medium	Medium	Medium to High	Low
Partial Employment– Group-Based Annuity	Medium	Low to Medium	High	Medium	Medium	Medium to High	Low

Table 17 *Continued*

Option	Criterion						
	Potential Funds Freed	*Employee Replacement Rate*	*Retirement Income Level*	*Administrative Feasibility*	*Legal Feasibility*	*Political Feasibility*	*Market Feasibility*
Continued Payment to Employee's Annuity	High	Low	No Interim Annuity	High	Medium	Medium	Low
Severence Payment Plus Continued Payment to Annuity	Medium to High	High	Medium (Little Change)	High	Medium	High	Medium
Liberalized Benefits Schedule	Low	Low	Medium (Little Change)	Low	High	High	Medium
Continuation of Perquisites	High per Acceptance --------- Low Probability of Acceptance	Low	Medium (Little Change)	High	High	High	Medium

relatively simple to administer; eligibility criteria are easily defined, benefits are easily calculated, and there are no such problems as finding part-time employment for the early retiree. Furthermore, as basically a one-time commitment to the retiree, the arrangement can be offered during limited time periods. However, it may be difficult to estimate the number of persons who will elect it. There should be few legal problems if employees volunteer for the option. Since the potential retiree will receive less than full salary at early retirement, there should be only moderate political difficulty with this option. There may be market-feasibility questions associated with this alternative. Some persons may resist accepting the option, fearing they may not be able to reemploy should their early-retirement income be insufficient.

Alternative 3: Individual-Based Early Annuity. Despite freeing fewer funds than the severance-payment scheme, this option may still free a moderate amount of funds, depending on how generous the supplemental payments are and whether cost-of-living adjustments are made. It also allows a medium employee-replacement rate. Because the supplement is paid for life, the retiree achieves a medium retirement income. A modest number of employees may elect this plan, but they may do so a few years earlier than they might under the lump-sum arrangement. Administrative difficulties include encouraging the "right" persons to take early retirement and correctly estimating the number of persons who will accept the option. Participation might be controlled somewhat by offering the option for limited periods. There are apparently no exceptional legal problems with the option, as long as employees voluntarily elect it. An institution will need legal advice on financing the supplemental payment. Political problems promise to be unexceptional but market feasibility may be an issue. Persons who fear they may not be able to obtain needed part-time employment after retirement may reject this option.

Alternative 4: Group-Based Early Annuity. Like the individual-based annuity, this scheme frees a moderate amount of funds per early retiree and allows a medium replacement rate. Since this alternative would offer lower-paid employees comparatively high annuities for retiring early, higher replacement rate among such employees might result. These early retirees would receive a moderate retirement income, and their supplemental payments would continue for life. There may be relatively few administrative problems with this option because the structure of its benefit schedule may encourage the "proper" employees to volunteer for early retirement. Nor should there be any exceptional legal problems, although the option may be less than politically acceptable; opposition to offering lower-paid employees larger supplemental annuities is predictable. Market feasibility may be a concern if the early retirees feel they may need to reemploy eventually. In some fields, reemployment possibilities are limited.

Alternative 5: Individual-Based Early Annuity with Partial Employment. This option, providing a greater early-retirement income to the retiree by combining part-time reemployment with the early annuity, frees only a low-to-medium amount of funds for hiring new employees. In most cases the funds freed will permit only a partial replacement. Savings might be centrally pooled and then reallocated, or they might be combined within a department to permit new hiring. Consequently, only a low-to-medium employee-replacement rate obtains. Although the employee's retirement income may be as high as his preretirement income, he must work part-time to obtain that income. Administering this option may be troublesome, for the institution will have to arrange for an employee to be retired and then rehired. Furthermore, this option does not always release the office space used by the part-time retiree; so, in fact, increased space demands may result. No unusual legal problems should arise. The major potential objection again should be the issue of paying someone to retire early. However, since the person is still employed on a part-time basis, this objection should be less severe as a political issue. In fact, this option is supported by persons who see it as an opportunity for employees to gradually enter retirement. Since the person is being reemployed, market feasibility is an issue; there must be something for the reemployed person to do. Many current faculty members have indicated that they would prefer early retirement with part-time reemployment. They have stated these preferences without a clear understanding of what the part-time job might be. Some recent incentive retirees who reemployed on a part-time basis wanted to teach small, graduate-level seminars, but their deans or chairmen wanted them to teach large introductory courses for undergraduates. Finding mutually agreeable part-time tasks may be difficult.

Alternative 6: Group-Based Early Annuity with Partial Employment. The evaluation of this option is similar to that of the partial employment plus individual-based annuity. A moderate amount of money is freed. There is a low-to-medium employee-replacement ratio. The employee receives a high retirement income. There are no unusual legal problems, and few political questions are raised; but there must be a market for the retiree's skills.

Alternative 7: Continued Annuity Contributions.   Since the only commitment the institution makes to the early retiree under this option is continued payment to his annuity fund, there is a great deal of money freed per retiree. However, few persons would elect this option, so its employee-replacement rate is low. The early retiree receives no early-retirement income. An easy alternative to administer because of its modest additional benefits and lack of salary supplements, this option might raise legal questions about the way in which the payments are made to the employee's annuity account. This is a politically feasible alternative because of its modest additional benefits. However, it may be acceptable only to employees who have the option of reemployment after retirement.

Alternative 8: Severance Payment with Continued Annuity Contributions.   Depending on the size of the severance payment under this option, there may be a medium-to-high level of funds freed per early retiree. The severance payment makes this an attractive option and should produce a high employee replacement ratio. The early retiree's early retirement income would be modest, varying with how the severance payment was made. The option should be easy to administer unless there is difficulty deciding the size of the supplemental payment. Its legal difficulties are related to the way in which the severance payment and annuity payments are made. There may be a few political problems if the severance payment is very large. Yet if the supplemental annuity is small, the option may appeal only to persons who are able to reemploy after retirement.

Alternative 9: Liberalized Benefits Schedule.   This option frees few funds because in most cases across-the-board benefit levels could not be raised high enough to cause many people to retire early.[1] Although a full salary line would be released for each early retiree, few new employees could be hired because so few persons would elect this option. There would be little change in the level of retirement income with this option because increasing funds for all retirees results in little increase for any particular person. Implementation difficulties would stem from the required modification of the entire retirement program, but there would be no exceptional legal problems. Since it would affect all employees, the change would be politically acceptable. Market feasibility might be an issue if the early retirees terminate a number of years before the mandatory age. Some persons would select this option only if they were confident of finding new work.

Alternative 10: Continuation of Perquisites. This alternative, though it would free close to 100% of salary funds per acceptance, may not be sufficiently attractive to encourage additional persons to retire early. Consequently, it would result in a low-employee-replacement rate. The option would have little or no effect on the size of one's annuity, except as it might reduce one's out-of-pocket expenditures. It would be easy to administer, since it would not affect the basic retirement plan. It promises few if any legal difficulties and should be politically acceptable because it applies to all retirees. Acceptance of the option may depend on the extent to which potential participants feel they may need to reemploy elsewhere.

POLICY CONSIDERATIONS

The decision to adopt an incentive early-retirement scheme can be made only after a careful analysis of institution-specific data and legal counsel. Although key issues would certainly include manpower needs and cost, there are other policies to be considered by colleges and universities needing to increase turnover and open the ranks to employees with new skills and qualifications.

Develop a Mechanism for Faculty Review and Evaluation. Were faculty members to engage in periodic review and evaluation, part of the need for mid-career change and early-retirement programs might be eliminated. The less-productive faculty members might recognize the desirability of changing careers while they still have the opportunity to do so. The eventual abolition of mandatory retirement will force colleges and universities to develop such mechanisms. One's right to continue in a given position will soon be established through the application of clearly stated criteria and procedures.

Provide Retirement and Financial Counseling. Prospective retirees, and young employees as well, need advice about their retirement program and other investment options. Workers need to save for retirement when they are young so that their funds have time to compound. Money added to a pension fund late in one's career simply does not have time to grow. A number of our respondents stated that they realized they should have sought pension and investment advice, but for some reason failed to do so. Institutions might advise current employees about various ways of preparing for retirement and offer information about the experiences of persons who followed these suggestions.

Disseminate Information about the Options. Getting the information about the alternatives to the right persons may not be easy. Employees tend to have little interest in their pension program until they near retirement. Although the availability of a special option might be publicized in general notices, a more direct approach may be necessary. Each eligible early retiree might be given a notification of his eligibility and a description of the early-retirement arrangement. Where possible, one office should handle the early-retirement arrangements and serve as sole contact for the early retirees. However, early retirement is both an academic and a personnel issue, so institutions may need to assign an academic officer to help retirement personnel process applications.

Assure Academic Units Some Return from Early Retirements. A college, school, or department might be reluctant to become involved in an early-retirement alternative if it would mean the loss of a faculty position. In some cases this loss is unavoidable, as when a unit is being reduced in size or eliminated. In cases where an early retiree will be replaced, academic units need to be assured they will receive funds with which to hire the replacement. Early retirees might be replaced on a one-to-one basis campus-wide while individual units still suffer losses. Gains and losses could be balanced in a campus-wide accounting procedure guaranteeing every academic unit a certain return on all early retirements during the year. If there were a central pool and a department had the opportunity to hire a great scholar, the department might borrow a position into which that person could be hired and give up a position later.

Do Not Necessarily Hire All Young Replacements. Consider how new appointments will affect faculty flow and replacement in years to come. In order to achieve flexibility in hiring, a central pool of reallocatable slots might be considered, and temporary appointments might be used to level fluctuations if the number of permanent full-time faculty members must remain constant.

Recognize Potential Contributions from Emeriti. Both mandatory-age and early retirees may desire to continue a relationship with the university. Although a physical facility may not be essential, there should be provisions made for emeriti who want to participate in projects and activities. A number of recent retirees said they would have liked to continue an association with their campus, and some were willing to carry committee assignments and the like.

Continue Certain Perquisites. An institution would not be making a mistake in the eyes of retirees if it provided a few nonpecuniary perquisites such as listings in the faculty directory, extended library privileges, campus parking, occasional secretarial services, office space, free faculty club membership, and reduced prices for cultural and sports events. Of course, the benefits would be a cost to the institution. But in most cases the cost would be minimal.

A WORD OF CAUTION

As mentioned in chapter 6, the provisions of the ADEA, ERISA and sections 403 (b) and 415 of the Internal Revenue Code require caution in the application of the alternatives outlined in this book. The ADEA prohibits involuntarily retiring an employee merely because of age. ERISA limits the amounts that may be added to an individual's pension account, and any institution desiring to supplement a retiree's annuity benefits should consult legal counsel about possible problems. Although public pension plans are exempt from ERISA, individuals are not exempt from provisions of the Internal Revenue Code. The way in which the supplement is purchased and paid to the employee should be reviewed by legal counsel.

POSTLUDE

There seem to be enormous advantages to a university's removing people who are tired, ineffective, or disaffected. Our research indicated that such persons do exist within academia, and mid-career and early-retirement options are ways to deal with their needs. Institutions must realize that although these options may open the faculty ranks to new employees with needed qualifications and skills, financial costs are involved. Persons considering changing careers and potential early retirees must understand that although these options may permit them to pursue new interests or to leave an undesirable situation, they may have to endure some financial loss. Nonetheless, it appears that mid-career change and early retirement can be beneficial to both institutions and individuals.

Obviously this conclusion does not suggest that most middle-aged academics should find new careers, nor does it suggest that all older academics should retire early. Finally, we do not suggest that academics be barred from continuing past the normal retirement age. But our research does point out that early retirees and persons who have made mid-career changes are generally faring well.

It is important that employees know about career options in order to make intelligent decisions about their futures. Similarly, institutions need to be aware of these alternatives so they can plan. There are unseen consequences of indentured labor—in particular, the effects of the alienated on other faculty members. Administered deftly, mid-career change and early-retirement options could respond to this problem as well as to some of the problems of the steady-state university.

NOTE

1. As noted earlier, across-the-board increases in early-retirement benefits may be very expensive. To make the increases large enough to encourage persons to retire earlier than planned would create dangerously high pension costs. See William C. Greenough and Francis P. King, "Is Normal Retirement at Age 65 Obsolete?" *Pension World* 13, no. 6 (June 1977): 35–36.

Appendix

GUIDE TO ADMINISTRATOR INTERVIEWS*

1. What is your basic mandatory-retirement provision?
2. What is the basic early-retirement provision?
3. What is the essence of the increased-benefits early-retirement arrangement?
   a. At whom is the arrangement aimed?
   b. What is the financial inducement?
   c. Is there a provision for cost-of-living adjustments?
   d. What inducements other than financial does the arrangement include?
   e. How were the benefit levels determined?
   f. What are the eligibility requirements?
      —years of service
      —minimum age
      —other
   g. Is it a formal or informal program?

---

* These questions were devised as an interview guide. The actual interviews were conducted as conversations, varying according to the unique circumstances of each institution.

4. What were the sources of the incentive early-retirement concept?

   a. Who were the key actors?

   b. What roles did they play?

5. Why was the concept originally considered?

6. What other early-retirement schemes were considered?

   a. Why were they dismissed?

   b. What inducements other than money were considered?

7. How many early retirements have you had under this arrangement?

8. What factors caused employees to agree to early retirement?

9. Were there any individuals who formally considered early retirement but did not take it? How many? Why did they not take the arrangement?

10. How was the policy announced/publicized/promoted? Generally, how were workers informed?

11. How were the early retirements handled?

    a. How extensive were the negotiations?

    b. Who were the key individuals involved in these negotiations?

    c. What were their roles?

12. Was special counseling provided potential early retirees?

13. What is your general evaluation of incentive early retirement?

    a. As a policy/program

    b. Administrative aspects

    c. Do superiors understand the program?

    d. Are the "right" people being selected?

    e. How might the program be improved?

    f. Beyond money, what should be part of an early-retirement program?

GUIDE TO EARLY RETIREE INTERVIEWS*

1. When did you retire? How old were you? How many years had you been employed by the university (company)?

---

* These questions were devised as an interview guide. The actual interviews were conducted as conversations, varying according to the unique circumstances of each individual.

2. What position did you hold at the time you retired? (*For faculty:* What was your academic field?)

3. What particular early-retirement arrangement was made in your case? How does this arrangement differ from normal mandatory or early retirement? In addition to direct benefits, what fringes were provided, such as medical coverage, health and life insurance, office and lab space, secretarial services, library and parking privileges, etc?

4. Had you always expected to retire when you did? If not, when did you originally expect to retire? When did you start to think seriously about early retirement?

5. What caused you to consider retiring early? Was there any special impetus in the last year or so before retirement?

6. Before you retired, did you talk with other persons about *when* you should retire?

7. How did you initially become aware of the early-retirement arrangement?

8. When, in relation to other events, did you and your immediate superior first discuss early retirement? Who first raised the issue of whether you should retire early? Why? What was the other's reaction?

9. Did you discuss early retirement with any other administrator (manager) before discussing it with your immediate superior? Who was it? When did this discussion take place? Who first raised the issue of whether you should retire early? Why? What was the other's reaction?

10. Did you feel any pressure from your superiors to retire early?

11. What was the administrative procedure for handling your early retirement? (Who was involved, and what roles did they play?)

12. How would you evaluate the administrative handling of your early retirement? (How satisfied are you with the way it was handled? What administrative changes do you feel are needed?)

13. How would you evaluate the provisions of the early-retirement arrangement? (How satisfied are you with those provisions? What changes or alternatives would you suggest?)

14. How satisfied are you now with your decision to retire early? What are your main reasons for feeling this way?

15. If you were able to make your decision of when to retire over again, under the same circumstances, what would you do? Retire sooner? Retire at about the same time? Retire later? Why?

16. Would you have retired even earlier if the conditions of the early-retirement arrangement had been different? If yes, what would have been the necessary conditions? Assuming these conditions could have been met, at what age might you have retired?

17. Beyond making financial plans, how did you prepare for early retirement? Did you find this useful? Other than financially, how would you prepare for early retirement if you were doing it over again?

18. What financial plans did you make for your retirement? How long before you retired did you begin to make these plans? Did you make these plans specifically for early retirement, or were they plans you would have made anyway? Did you change, or reevaluate, your financial plans when you decided to retire early? In what way?

19. Did you receive any formal counseling about early retirement? If so, did you find it beneficial? If not, do you feel you needed any?

20. Have you worked for pay since your initial retirement from the university (company)? What was the nature of this work? How much time was committed to it?

21. Are you now working for pay? If so, are you satisfied with the amount you are now working, or would you rather be working more or less? Why? If you are not now working for pay, would you like to have some kind of paid employment? Why?

22. What types of income do you presently have? Which sources of income provide your primary support?

23. How does your present standard of living compare with your standard of living before retirement? How does it compare with what you expected it to be?

24. What are your current leisure, professional, and volunteer activities? How do they relate to what you were doing before you retired? Are you continuing any of the professional activities you were engaged in before you retired? What are your plans for the next few years?

25. Compared with your life before retirement, how happy are you with your life now? Why?

26. Do you know of any colleagues who considered and then decided against retiring early? If yes, why did they decide against it?

27. What do you feel are the essential ingredients for a successful early retirement?

Index